Writing Dialogue

TOM CHIARELLA

STORY PRESS
CINCINNATI, OHIO

Writing Dialogue. Copyright © 1998 by Tom Chiarella. Printed and bound in the United States of America. All rights reserved. No part of this book may be reproduced in any form or by any electronic or mechanical means including information storage and retrieval systems without permission in writing from the publisher, except by a reviewer, who may quote brief passages in a review. Published by Story Press, an imprint of F&W Publications, Inc., 1507 Dana Avenue, Cincinnati, Ohio 45207. (800) 289-0963. First edition.

Story Press Books are available from your local bookstore or direct from the publisher.

02 01 00 99   5 4 3 2

Library of Congress Cataloging-in-Publication Data

Chiarella, Tom.
    Writing dialogue / Tom Chiarella.
        p.   cm.
    Includes index.
    ISBN 1-884910-32-7 (pbk. : alk. paper)
    1. Authorship. 2. Fiction—Technique. 3. Dialogue. I. Title.
PN218.C618   1997
808.3'96—dc21   97-36717
                                                                      CIP

Designed by Clare Finney

For Hendrie, my teacher.

ACKNOWLEDGMENTS

I have dedicated this book to my friend and teacher Don Hendrie, who died several years ago. He left my life quite suddenly—the way teachers do—when *I* moved on. After that he got sick, and we lost touch, and the next thing I knew I had never told him the things I needed to say. He taught me in much the same way I hope this book teaches. He had expectations. He demanded commitment. He made me laugh. At times, he puzzled me. I never knew what he wanted for me, except that he expected me to be responsible for myself and to write hard. Good watchwords. I appreciate the chance Hendrie took on me, the work he did for me. Such gruff lessons! I miss him.

Still, it would be irresponsible for me not to recognize all of my teachers. Some people say you can't teach writing. I just don't buy it. These people worked wonders on me. In my largely miserable high school experience, I had several terrific English teachers who helped to fashion in me a sense of voice. I knew them only as Mr. Fleche, Mr. Turk and Mr. Fahy. In college and later in graduate school, I was lucky enough to have worked with a number of great teachers of writing and art: Guy Berard, Phil Larsen, Roger Bailey, Joe David Bellamy, Allen Wier, Tom Rabbitt, Chase Twichell and Valerie Martin.

Beyond that I would like to acknowledge the help and guidance of my friend Barbara Bean, my colleague at DePauw. We teach together and I am damned lucky for it.

Wouldn't I be a particular fool if I were not to thank my students, particularly Mimi Lottes, for their patience, their help and their friendship? They are a good reason to go to work each day, and there are some truly fine writers among them.

I am much thankful to all the members of DePauw's English department, a uniquely generous and gifted group. Thanks, too, to the many
other friends who circle my life here at DePauw: Gigi and Bill Fenlon,
David Newman, and Steve Timm among them.

The institutional support from DePauw has been a great help to
my work as a writer and as a teacher, in particular the Amy Braddock
Fund and the John and Janice Fisher Fund for Faculty Development.

This book would be nothing without Jack Heffron, who offered the
advice of a fine writer and thoughtful editor. Every publishing house
should be so lucky as to have someone like him.

Finally, Gus, Walter and Lisa deserve my grandest round of thanks.
Just typing their names here makes me dizzy with love. They are my
family. It is to them I owe everything I know about listening and
talking.

CONTENTS

INTRODUCTION

Do me a favor. Pick nearly any two books of fiction from the shelves of a library or bookstore. Read a few pages of each, and compare the treatment of dialogue. Odds are, you'll find that the two are miles apart. One writer is burying himself in dialect, while the other writer uses almost no spoken words at all. Or one writer's characters sound like fortune cookies, while another one's sound exactly the way your mother did when she was chasing you around with that wooden spoon when you were six. Who has it right? One thing is clear: Every writer grapples with dialogue in her own way, and for every reader there are certain writers who get dialogue "right."

What's the secret? Well, if I had the answer, I'd put it in a spice bottle and charge you by the gram. Practice, I guess. Keep writing. To that sort of advice, I grant you my own first line of dialogue: "Thanks for nothing, babe!"

There is no secret, except to learn how to *trust* the language you hear, to learn to *hear* the people around you and to *expose yourself* to as many voices (and techniques) as possible.

This book should help you with some of that. It works to show you ways to relearn listening, to break down the dialogue you come across in your own life and in your own reading. It will find ways to help you generate dialogue to lead you to stories and make existing dialogue work better within your work. It attempts to help your dialogue sound more like "real life" without losing the flavor of your craft.

What it won't do is set you up with rule upon rule. I have one rule and one piece of advice. I'll give them to you here, so long as you're browsing. The rule: Above all else, work. The advice: Question the need for rules in matters such as these.

This book is an attempt to provide you with a series of examinations of what makes "good" dialogue good, and how to make "bad" dialogue better. The first chapter starts out by looking at the dialogue you hear, the second moves to the dialogue you read and the third, fourth and fifth ask you to examine the dialogue you write, suggesting specific methods and patterns for editing. The next two chapters attempt to show you ways to use the dialogues you come across and the dialogues you create to lead you to new stories. The final chapter tries to answer the nuts-and-bolts questions of dialogue, including format, punctuation and the use of dialogue tags.

I've tried to make it entertaining. I hope you'll hear a little of my own voice in the middle of all of this. At times, I'm sure, my prejudices show through; at others, you'll catch a bit of my attitude. But what's a conversation without a little of each of those?

So, lots of energy and no hard-and-fast rules. Well, maybe a few hard-and-fast rules. Use them if they make sense to you. And since, in these pages, I set forth an argument for putting a premium on economy, I ask that you turn the page and start the dialogue.

ONE

LISTENING, JOTTING, CROWDING

The world is crowded with voices. While we can retreat to our silences from time to time, most of us are called on to speak and listen for the better part of every day. From the beginning of our lives we listen, in preparation to speak. As infants, we first listen to the world, to the intentional and unintentional prattle of the adults, before we speak. Later, given voice in the world, we speak and find that sometimes we are listened to, other times not. So we try different strategies. We recite. We give reports. We greet one another. We yell. We joke. We cajole. We blurt out secrets. We lie. We tell stories.

If there's anything you're an expert on, it's your own voice. I'm not referring to the sound of it, though presumably no one sounds as much like you as you do (unless you're Johnny Carson, and then everyone thinks he sounds more like you than you). I'm referring to your voice as a reflection of who you are, of your consciousness. The words you choose, the idioms you select, the metaphors you rely on, consciously or unconsciously, this is your voice as I define it. It is you. They can put you in jail. They can throw you in the hole. They can soundproof the room. They can even take away your cigarettes! But you still have your voice.

So what's so hard about writing dialogue? It's just speaking, right? Well, the truth is, writing dialogue is not all that hard. I can teach you ways to fill up pages with the stuff. There are many writers who do it exceptionally well, propelling plot lines along, carving entire scenes out of dialogue. One would think it's like setting up a microphone in front of the world. You create a character. As you write, you begin to know her, until you feel, finally, that you understand her. When she speaks, you might expect to feel that it's like turning on a faucet, that the words ought to flow out of her in a torrent. Only if you're lucky. Whether they do or not, you'll find that writing dialogue is *not* a matter of including everything that's said. This is a physical and intellectual impossibility. Writing dialogue is a craft that demands that you *shape* what a character says so that it's representative, artful, revealing and honest.

Good dialogue is like no other part of a story in that it can, and it ought to, give some sense of being an event unto itself. Good dialogue lends the readers a sense that it is happening outside the writer's control, while clearly it is anything but outside his control. When dialogue slides in between the quotes, it says to the reader that there's another voice at work here, another source. It's an illusion for the most part; though of all the elements of fiction, good dialogue comes closest to reflecting the world accurately, if only for a flash.

So you have a voice. Start writing dialogue, right? Well, no. Not surprisingly, I'm going to ask you to start the way you began all those years ago, back when people used to carry you around in their arms, back when they encouraged you to play with the wooden spoons as if they meant something, back before you were such an expert on your own voice, Mr. Smartypants.

I want you start out by listening.

JABBER

If you really listen to yourself talk, you might find that you sound like a moron. I know I do. On the morning I started this book, I did what I always do when I talk to my students about writing dialogue: I listened. I spent an entire day listening to myself.

You can't write convincing, compelling dialogue in fiction unless you like to listen. I'm not talking about listening to the vireos chirping in your redbud or the Great Northern rumbling along the north side tracks either (although these sorts of sounds surely ought to find their way into your fiction). And I'm not talking about listening for "real meaning" either; no deconstruction allowed, no groping for metaphors. This sort of listening is not about sounds, not yet anyway. It's not about paradigms or constructs. I'm telling you to listen to yourself. This is about the ways *you* use words. Now this is hard to do. Harder than you might imagine. When you really listen to yourself, you can't help shaping what you say. When that happens, you won't sound like yourself, defeating the point of the exercise outright. You'll find you have to control your self-awareness so the entire day isn't spent in some sort of meaningless charade, you rasping like Christian Slater or popping words out like Cary Grant.

The key to this sort of listening is a method of recording. You could use a tape recorder—there are uses for tape recorders, which I'll get to—but for this exercise, I recommend writing everything down. It's possible to do it as you go, pausing after each sentence to record, but the self-consciousness question comes up, not to mention the dirty looks. You have to keep people around you unaware so you can fall into the normal patterns. At the same time, you have to stay aware, to listen and find time to record.

Scribbling in the Notebook

Since it's awkward to end a conversation by scribbling down the last few words, I decided to keep a mental tally until my next free moment, during which I did any necessary scribbling in a red spiral notebook, which I carried with me everywhere I went. I didn't worry about what anybody else said. Only me. I didn't worry about noting the time of conversations or to whom I was speaking. So I have no idea when, or why, I said, "Have you taken care of your dog's nails yet?" But, late that morning, I did. It's in the notebook.

What was I left with at the end? Various discoveries. I was distressed to find that I use the word "yup" all the time. I found that I am no artist when it comes to the passing line. By this I mean the sort of thing you say to someone as you stride past. "How's it going?" qualifies. (Six times.) "What's up?" was my distinct favorite when I was younger, but has now diminished in frequency to no more than once or twice a day (in my spiral notebook it appears only once). How could I use a word like "howdy"? (I do though, a lot it seems.) I found that I have a series of more personalized greetings for those who turn square to me (things such as "Yo" and "Good morning, all!"). I discovered that I have an awful habit of calling people by their full names in lieu of a greeting, as if this were some sort of hail, some new information for us both ("Lynn Gram!" "David Newman!") In all, I said "hello" eleven times, nine of them when answering the phone, once to my secretary and once to my son, while trying to break his gaze from the television ("Hello? Why aren't your socks on your feet?"). Twice I used the catchy "Y-ello" instead. (Lord.) I also used a sound, something like "uh" but my own personalized "uh," more like "eh" or "eah"—a sound that seemed to punctuate any compound complex sentence I was forced to put together, as if I had to—eah—grope for each clause like a man trimming a bush one branch at a time.

A typical page in the notebook looked like this, with each line being something I said.

Howdy	Oh yes
Jimmy Bell	Gordon Walters
Howdy	Just checking
Shoe boy	Yesterday
Straight up	Put that in your book
Vertical	I'll be here until three eh
I'm telling you	after that I have to get the
Hi	and I don't have the car
Hi	seat shit
I didn't. Not at all	No not really I could be
What's up	ready at quarter of
No, eh	I don't think so
No kidding	Not really
I was playing poker	Wayne said it, you know it's
Late	true
A lot	How's Mary
Yup	I got it
Yup	I am in hell
Three pages	Howdy

That was about fifteen minutes of talking, I think, to eight or ten different people. I believe most of this particular section occurred in the halls outside my office, with my co-workers or with my students. Whenever I ducked back inside my office, I scribbled in my spiral. Whenever I felt I was slipping into Cary Grant-speak, I just stopped talking, or found an excuse to go record in my spiral.

I was able to keep up with this from the time I woke until I went into my first class (about five hours), and I started again after my last class too.

What does it leave me with? Where's the connection to fiction? Well, I now realize that I jabber. I chatter on. I am, as I said, a wellspring of clichés and euphemisms. These are the very words and phrases I worry about most in my student's work and in my own. This sort of stuff has no place in fiction. In class, I say things like these: Avoid clichés. Don't let the dialogue rattle on. Compress. Don't lose the tension of a dialogue. And yet, when I talk, I sound like everything I am warning against. I sound, more disturbingly for me, like a prattling moron.

But sometimes jabber tells a story of its own. Return to my spiral notebook page. What can you draw out of it? Lots of greetings. Those took place in the halls of my office building, as I've already said, where I run into lots of students and fellow teachers. It's also because I teach at a small Midwestern college, where everyone seems to say hello no matter what mood they're in. These are matters of context, of setting. You also find very few complete sentences. Most of the exchanges are punchy, three or four words and no more. This too comes from context—the halls of a college between classes—but it also has to do with character. It's what I like to do. I float around, give people grief, then move on. Does everyone talk like this? Lord, no. But there was a time when I thought I spoke in full sentences. I've since found that, at one time or another, most of us don't. Finally, although I didn't punctuate the jabber, if you look closely at it, you'll see some rhythms, and in those you see my own tensions and stresses: I was worried about picking up my children; I was telling a student he had to give me three pages, no less; I was late, feeling overwhelmed. You see this in the incomplete sentences too.

Context, character, rhythm, tension and stresses. You'll be hearing a lot on these matters. I find them within a twenty-minute segment of my own life. You can too. It's worth studying the way you talk, the ways people around you talk. In these you can find the shapes of life. And by listening, you can begin the process of shaping dialogue to suit your fiction.

LISTENING: TUNING IN AND TUNING OUT

Listening is not easy. We train ourselves to tune out language. To get through a day during which you move from point A to point B in our culture, you have to slip in the word filter. Forget what *you* say for a moment. Button your lip. But think about all the words you hear. Deejays on the radio. Paging calls at the airport. The calls of a waitress to her short-order man. The voice at the drive-through. The two guys in the row behind you in the theater, the ones who just won't shut up. Not to mention the guy at work, the one who goes on about rebuilding an engine while you try to carve out ten silent minutes to eat your tuna salad on rye.

To live our lives without going bonkers, we run a sort of white noise over the top of all of this. We tune out, and we are trained to do so from the very start of our lives. We treat words the way we might treat junk mail or a forgotten toy. Words become scenery. The jabber of a cartoon on the television is a part of the background, even if it is in another room, part of the scenery in a home, the sort of voice we live with, the words no more than pulses, sounds without meaning.

Not me, you say. Maybe you live in the mountains, with your wolf, to whom you speak three words a day. Maybe you just boil the coffee in a tin pot and then chop wood for winter. At night you might lie down and say a blessing. Then you go to sleep without having said twenty words. No tuning out for you. No rush and razzle of contemporary life. Congrats! But I still think you should go buy a spiral. In fact, drive all the way into Butte, go to a mall and buy it at a chain drugstore. While you're at it, try *not* tuning a few words out. You'll be looking for the earplugs before you know it ("Aisle seven, on the right, next to the swimmer's ear drops. Right down there. Keep going. A little farther. There. Right in front of you. There. Look down. Yes. There. Okay.").

I have a sister-in-law, whom I like very much, who is hard of hearing. Every Christmas, I sit next to her on the couch during the festivities and find that she can hear me only when I shout directly into her ear. She won't wear her hearing aids. This past year, I asked her why. She told me that they work too well. "Hear too much," she said. "I hear everything—*every*thing—when those are in my ears, every word that's spoken within forty yards. I hear people's stomachs. Everybody's shouting. And people talk so much. So many wasted words. Jabber. Jabber. Jabber."

It's a sad fact really that we are forced to filter out so much in contemporary life. We are assaulted by images from the moment we are born. No argument here. But we are in a hailstorm of words too. And to survive, we have to filter, tune out, stop listening. But to write fiction, you have to listen. You have to tune in. Eavesdrop. Take note. But you also have to listen carefully. Select. Edit. Pare down. This is tuning out. These are opposite sorts of disciplines, but they are part of the same act. I guarantee it. Think of the world as if it were a short-band radio, which you can crank up when you need to. Indeed, you need to be able to turn up the power on your listening abilities to catch even the most stray signals on the most obscure channels. There are several ways to do that.

Jotting

First thing, start a journal. A spiral notebook like the one I used in the earlier exercise about listening will be fine, but it should be small enough to carry around with you. I have one I keep in the glove compartment of my truck. While I don't slip it into my pocket every time I leave the truck, I have taken it with me to meetings, malls and at least one county fair. Jot in it. Listen for good fragments. Try to catch oddball phrases.

How do you do this? You have to be comfortable eavesdropping for one thing. Sometimes you just get lucky. I play in a regular basketball game at noon, and the court is situated alongside two others in the middle of an indoor track. Before the game starts, I stretch my Achilles tendon like there's no tomorrow. I find this is quiet time for me, so I listen. A day or two ago, while the game was shaping up on the court, two or three groups of people were walking or running around the track. One couple caught my attention—two women, dressed in street clothes, walking. I could tell they worked in an office from the way they dressed and that they were fairly serious about the walking from the look of their shoes. Normally I would pass right by these two without a thought. Prime candidates for the word filter from the get-go. But as I stretched, I found they were easy to watch, cruising the far side of the track. One of the women, the heavier one, was doing most of the speaking, and the other one was listening. Soon they passed out of my line of vision and I started answering the hoots from the court—"Let's Go!" "Shake it out!" "Skin up!"—then as I passed from my stretching spot, I found that I was walking behind the women, as they had circled the track. And for a moment, I was close enough to hear one of them say, "That's what's funny about all of it."

Having seen even at a distance that it was a fairly animated story, I wanted to hear the rest, and as I was directly behind them, I took a step or two along the track, pretending to limber up some more. "When he took that day job," the woman said. Then no more. Someone from the court bounced me a ball. I caught it and walked behind, now fully tuned in. The woman went on. "Well, she was over there all morning just doing her business in that nasty little trailer."

The other woman howled. "Yucky!" she said.

At that point, I made a key mistake in my listening exercise: I casually bounced the basketball once. They became aware of my presence crowding them on the track. They fell silent and I slipped back, still disturbingly interested in that nasty little trailer, begrudgingly joining the game. Later, when I was in my truck, I took my spiral in hand and wrote down their exchange. I made a note about where I heard it, but not a long one.

> Two women, circling: When he took that day job, she was over there doing her business in that nasty little trailer. Yucky.

This is jotting. I do it all the time. It's not exact recording. It's capturing a phrase or words and a circumstance. Nothing more. It's a fine starting point for writing dialogue. Just grab the words for whatever reason, and slap them down so they stay with you.

Why did I write these words? There's a story in them, of course. The nasty trailer, the marriage falling apart, the guy shifting jobs, the woman and her "business." That's good stuff, and I'm going to suggest throughout this book that good fiction can be created out of things overheard. But for me the news about the woman, the trailer, the "business" was not as interesting as the response it got from the other woman circling the track: "Yucky."

Why? Let's say you've never heard this exchange and you're writing a story. One character, Linda, is about to tell the other, say Helen, this juicy piece of gossip.

> "When he took that day job," Linda said, pressing forward, "she started going over there to that nasty trailer every morning, doing her business."

Think like the writer now. What can Helen say? The news is out there. One choice would be to allow her response to invite the dialogue to slide forward, inviting another bit of news. This is so easy it's almost mindless.

> "You're kidding," Helen said.
> "No! Really?" Helen said.
> "I can't believe it," Helen said.
> "Wow," Helen said.

I'm a realist. Writing dialogue is tough, and sometimes you just have to let the characters say something that allows things to trip forward. After all, Linda will probably have more to say. But Helen's responses above are just jabber. If a writer uses one of these lines, or one like it, he's just using jabber to indicate the back and forth of a conversation. Back and forth, like a metronome. I would argue that this is not how most conversation runs, for one thing, but frankly I think this type of thoughtless response forces the reader to slip on the word filter.

What a waste that is. Think about it. You invite a reader into your story. The fact that you wrote it says you want the reader to pay attention to your words. So why let wasted words slip right into the mouths of your characters?

"Yucky" is a better response than any of those I suggested. The woman on the track could have said, "You're kidding," and I wouldn't have been surprised. Frankly I tuned in at that moment because the word "yucky" related so much of what she was thinking. It might have been the nasty trailer she was responding to or the woman's infidelity or her doing "her business" while her husband was at work. And while it's not a word I used a lot before (although now I do use it, having since test-piloted it into conversations, which, later on, I'll recommend to you), it is a word that might describe a reaction to all three of these bits of news. (In a trailer. Yucky! Infidelity. Yucky! Doing her business. Yucky!) Beyond that, it seemed like a word a kid would use, a word far too young for those two women circling my basketball game. And, notably, I think it was a funny response to what might be called bad news.

If I hadn't had my spiral in my glove box, I likely wouldn't have thought to write that down. But I'm in the habit because I make myself jot lots of things. A writer has many uses for a notebook, or a journal, uses that are well documented and well reasoned by writers far more accomplished than I. You should take notes vigorously. On everything. No argument here. But I'm telling you something a little more focused. I'm talking about jotting. Make a note on the physical circumstance, but keep it brief. No more than three words.

By the fountain:
What's the flower? What's the symbol?

Running:
No. No. No. I'm. I'm. I'm not.

On a plane:
That's why it always goes this way.
So true.
And weddings are usually a disaster because of it.

New York:
I take photographs. But I'm not a photographer.
Per se.
Right. Not per se.
Right.

A dark hallway, after closing:
Are you with me?
Right here.
I mean.
Yes, I follow.
Cause it's important.
I get you.

These are stray jots. I culled them from several spirals, recorded over several years. I heard these on trips. I heard these during my lunch hour, as people passed by. Often I was one of the speakers.

There were moments when I got everything I could and it was enough, and others when I only wrote down part of what I heard and it was too much. When I look back at these, I am pulled right back into the moment. The jotting marked "New York" is from a time I was in a baggage carousel at LaGuardia and these two guys were talking while staring at the flight arrivals, about as interested in one another as two cows in a field. The lines marked "after closing" were a conversation I overheard in the halls of my office building between two janitors as they sat in the student lounge on their break. They didn't know I was there, around the corner, using the echoes of the hall to help me listen, but I was, and I remember I wrote it down because I thought they sounded like two cat burglars.

There are plenty of these jots I don't even remember hearing. The one at the fountain seems peculiar to me, almost contrived and at the same time just incomplete enough to be real. It could be that I made it up. Or that I heard part of it and made up the rest. Or that I overheard it incorrectly. It doesn't matter now. That's the point. By writing it down, whether it happened or not, whether I got it exactly right or not, I've given myself something to work with, something to drum through my head. These are rhythms. There is context within them. These are my jots. A few of them anyway. I got them by listening to the world. I got them, quite frankly, by crowding the people around me. That's the thing. To jot well, you have to crowd nicely.

CROWDING

Maybe you don't hear so well. Maybe you don't notice things people say. Maybe you like to have your space and think you should give others theirs as well. You don't want to get close. You don't want to crowd. It makes you uncomfortable. You're sure it makes others uncomfortable too. No crowding for you. Hey, quit whining. You're working here. Do it in small steps if you have to, but crowd.

There are lots of ways to crowd. You don't have to break laws to do it. I insist that you don't have to make anyone uncomfortable either. There are certain places where you can't avoid overhearing conversations. As you can guess, these make good natural starting points. Subways are super (but notice how hard it is to hear, and notice how little people really say there). The baggage carousel at the airport, as noted above, is one of my favorite spots. Airports in general are nice places to crowd. There you can put up a newspaper and lean back to hear the guy in the row of seats behind you apologizing to his children for leaving them to go skiing. Or you can lean against a wall and listen to a family waiting for one grandmother or the other to step through the gate. People tend to resolve things at airports, or try to, if only temporarily. It's natural. These moments can be tense or sad or jubilant. They are nothing if not charged. You have to rely on that. The airport is a natural place to crowd, and it's easy because you can always pretend to be preoccupied with your own set of tensions, your own departures or double-parks or delays.

There are other nice spots. Diners, with their back-to-back booths. Parks. Barbecue joints. Movie theaters, before the show. Lines at the bank. Baseball games. Airport limousines. Hotel lobbies. Convenience stores. Oil change places. Museums. Post offices.

How do you do it? Take one step closer. Lean in slightly. Make yourself as quiet as you can and stare straight ahead. It's important to remember that when I use the term "crowding," I do not mean physical crowding. I mean conscious listening. I mean stealing the words from the air around you. It's a different relationship to the world. It is, I believe, one facet of the writer's relationship to the world. You are tuning in.

In this case you, the listener, are nothing more than a recorder. A machine. Picture yourself as an inanimate object. Minimize movement. Pretend to be thinking hard about something. That way no matter what people say—and there will come times when they test the waters to see if you're listening—you won't show any reaction, so you won't stop them from talking. You won't interrupt the rhythm of what they say, not any more than any stray element of public conversation.

Must you crowd only in public? Of course not. Public conversation is only one sort of dialogue. But it's hard to learn to tune in when you've spent your whole life tuning out. So I'm asking you to change the way you think about public space. Make it yours. Do it consciously. Do it quietly.

STEALING FROM HOME

Do you have to go public? Does everything one hears and says within a story have to mimic the rhythms of public conversation? Don't you speak differently at home than you do in an airport? Doesn't private conversation have a rhythm of its own?

Of course it does. My point here isn't to teach you a way of speaking. That's not my purpose anywhere in this book. I'm trying to show you how to pick up on what makes for good dialogue within a story. I'm asking you to listen to the dialogues around you, the ones you've been tuning out for years, to see how they differ from what you expected.

The art of private conversation is one you've spent a lifetime working on. You probably think you have a good handle on it. In stories, most conversation is private; that is, it's directed between characters who know something of each other, or expect to. The pace and rhythm of the dialogue is completely tied up in issues like character, setting, the level of tension and even the structure of the story. These are issues we'll be dealing with throughout this book; they're ones that you'll deal with as you write stories.

But the principles of crowding and jotting still apply, no matter how well you think you know your family, your husband, your best friend, your favorite uncle. The danger comes most often when you start writing a dialogue thinking, *I know exactly how this is going to go.* No surprises for you generally means no surprises for the reader. If you aren't hearing your characters, you're treating them like furniture. Each dialogue has to create itself, even if it has jobs to do (like resolving a conflict or delivering some key slice of exposition).

So listen at home too. Crowd and jot. Remember that you are part of a tissue of life within these private contexts. How do you greet each other? What catchphrases does your family, peer group, etc., favor? Are they private too, making sense only within the group? Or are they drawn from the outside world? Do you finish sentences for one another? Does one person become more talkative in groups? Less? Is one person shy and demure in public but foulmouthed once you're alone in the car? These are rhythms. They help you create character, and in the end, stories. Your family, your private life, your past—that's where you find them. You'd be a fool not to tap into these things.

Again, I urge you to be self-conscious about it. Don't just lurk in the shadows with your ballpoint and your spiral. Challenge your own preconceptions. Surprise the people around you. Get a rise out of them. Confront them with language. Walk downstairs and greet everyone with, "Hi-ho!" Or whisper your responses to all questions. Or better yet, whisper the same word. Try something like "monkeys." Don't push it. Just see if they surprise you in return, or if they are threatened, or if they threaten to commit you. Then work your way out of it, get to your spiral and write down what they said and how they said it.

Private lives are as important as public lives when it comes to the rhythms of dialogue. In both cases, the key to starting out is listening to break your own preconceptions of the way people speak, of the things they say and of the way they say it. Listen until you are surprised. Then listen some more. This time you'll be surprised sooner. And sooner still the next time. You'll find that stories are brushing past you in hallways, at the hot dog stand. Then you have to select. Then you have to pick and choose. That's another step, but for the writer, there are far worse fates than being swamped with ideas, being struck down by rhythms.

EXERCISES

1. Listen to yourself. Spend the day recording everything you say. In the order you say it. Scroll out the whole day, recording everything you say, in a line-by-line fashion. Try to grab every sound. Every utterance. Don't leave out the little things, such as "hi" and "how are you" and "fine." Just record. Don't worry about punctuation. Or contexts. Don't note where you were or what time of day it was. Don't skip lines to indicate time passing or direction of dialogue. Just record from the moment you get up until the moment you go to bed. Don't explain it to anyone; don't even reveal it to anyone. Steal a few moments here and there to jot.

You should find that this gets easier as the day goes on. If you have a job where you talk all the time, you might want to buy a small pocket recorder and let it run whenever you speak. Either way, there are two keys to this exercise: (1) Record everything in writing. Even if you tape parts of your day, take the time at the end to transcribe it into your spiral. (2) Shape nothing; that is, don't let yourself change the way you normally speak. When you find yourself doing this, stop talking. Just shut up. I think this is the hardest thing to remember when writing fiction.

Save this recorded day as a document or database. Type it up line by line. We'll use it again and again.

2. Lug yourself to a public place where you can crowd. If you live close enough, try the airport. But you could go anywhere people travel

in bunches. Bus stations. Malls. Restaurants. Forget fiction for a moment. Go where the people are, even if you hate sitting in Denny's for more than the time it takes to drink a cup of joe. Remember my rule. To jot well, you must crowd nicely. Take your spiral. Take your time. Move like a special agent. Try sitting in various spots. At first, jot down everything. Shoot for the first three exchanges you hear between two people. Once you have that, move on. Check your watch, get up and go. No matter how good or bad the exchange was. That way you won't have to worry about getting punched in the nose for eavesdropping. Record ten or fifteen of these exchanges, using one word to describe the context, followed by a colon, then the exchange.

When finished, look over what you have. Perhaps you see stories galore. Choose one and run with it. Don't wait for me to tell you another thing about writing dialogue. You've been triggered. You can't ask for much more from the world around you. Go and write. Then come back and read chapter two. But perhaps you got nothing. Just a bunch of how-do-you-do's and some exec rambling about the annual reports. Go back. This time be more conscious of whom you choose to crowd and why: The guy with the mohawk, the one carrying the car seat with an infant in it. Or the old couple, clearly arguing about a scarf. What about the two businessmen, nervously tightening up as they approach their rental car? Move in, brush by. Grab what you can. If you've gone this far, you'll be able to grab a few words in an odd context.

Again, hold on to these. We will use them again.

3. Script your day. Before you go to bed, write in order everything you are going to say the next day. Picture the day clearly: getting up, the breakfast conversation, parking the car, passing familiar faces in the hall. The next day, stay with the script. Risk disruption. Stop when things don't make any sense to you or the person you're talking to, but stop only at the last minute, only after you've stretched it as far as you possibly can. How much of the dialogue you ran into was predictable? How far did you get before someone said something you didn't expect? What was the element of change? Take note of what you were able to expect and what came out of nowhere. One of the mistakes writers make is to assume that there's a predictability to the everyday. Mundane conversations can be full of particulars of change. Think how much your conversation changes with something as simple as

the weather. Or the news. Even the unpredictable moods of those around you. The point here is not to declare that we can't script our lives. You know that. Still, when you start a scene, you'll have a script like this somewhere in place, full of assumptions about where the dialogue should go. The point of this exercise is to make a script that must fight predictability as clearly as your life does every day.

4. Try a little guerrilla dialogue at home. Think of a question that can't be answered easily. Something like "How much does your liver weigh?" or "How many garbage cans are there in the whole world?" Ask it of everyone you know. Press each of them to be as precise as possible, but don't explain your curiosity, even after you get an answer. Fend them off. Confound them by not giving in. List their responses. Record the answers, yes, but take note of their reactions. What questions do they follow with? How do they word them? Are they threatened? Thrilled? Puzzled to the point where they throw up their hands? What do they think you're getting at? What are they worried about?

5. Using a long, overheard dialogue, such as the one from exercise two, remove all punctuation and lowercase all the letters. Just make the exchanges clear by skipping a line after each one. Hand the pages to two friends to read aloud. Tell them nothing about the circumstance or physical context of the conversation. As they read, follow along reading your own copy of the dialogue. Keep a pen handy. Mark their pauses. Underline the points where the readers get fouled up, where one sentence gets pushed into the next. Now punctuate the dialogue using the rhythms of their reading as your guide. Forget sentence structure. Don't fret the fragments. Just think rhythm.

TWO

THE DIRECTION OF DIALOGUE

EXAMPLES AND POSSIBILITIES

Writing dialogue is so much about the energy and direction of the story at hand that many of the things a writer does are intuitive. A turn here. An exclamation. A silence. I'll often hear experienced writers say they've developed an "ear" for dialogue. The implication is that dialogue exists in the world and writers merely record, with good writers—those with the "ear" for it—recording a little more clearly. The truth is, it's not solely about recording, or listening, but about shaping.

When I speak of the energy and direction of a story, I am referring to its tone and emotion (energy) and tension (direction). Writers craft, or shape, patterns of energy and direction in dialogue. In many ways these become the signatures of their dialogue, the things that make the voices of their characters recognizable and sustainable. Writers may have an ear for dialogue, but what they work with is a voice, shaped and charged by the needs of story. What your character says is directed by the needs of the story.

Classifying dialogue by techniques can be troublesome. Writers don't work that way. Most writers I know despise the very act of naming the things they do. It makes them too self-conscious to think of the patterns they create as they create them. I'm going to do some of that here, but only for the purposes of comparison. You should be looking for the occasional pause, the turn, the reversal, the silence that defines each of these moments. Naming the patterns is unimportant; reading to uncover them is a worthy task.

Thus you must be willing to take dialogue apart to look at what makes it tick. As you read, be willing to isolate moments within a dialogue. Highlight them in your book. Dog-ear the pages. Tear out a page and tape it to the wall above your computer. The idea is to take the dialogue on its own terms, to isolate the specific techniques the writer uses, before returning to the story as a whole to examine the dialogue's function in the larger context.

Begin by looking for the general tension of the dialogue. Some beginning writers confuse tension with conflict, assuming it comes and goes depending on whether characters agree or disagree. Tension is more like the energy between charged particles. It's always there, even when two people agree. Think of two cars traveling a reasonable distance apart from one another along an interstate at sixty-five miles an hour. Safe distance. Same direction. Same speed. No tension, right? Wrong. We all know it only takes one little bump in the road, one touch of the brakes, a doe in the headlights for everything to be completely and suddenly redefined. So you might start by looking for those three qualities when gauging the tension of your dialogue: direction, speed and distance (or separation).

TENSION IN DIALOGUE

How do I apply all this talk of direction, speed and distance to a dialogue?

Set two characters up in a blank room—that is, a bare stage, a void, a place not yet defined. Now make a decision. One of them wants something. The other does not have it, or can not get it. How will the first get it, if not by speaking? He must move in the direction of his desire.

> 1: Give it to me.

The direction here is clear and declarative. It's a palpable tension. Surely, you can see that this addresses a need in a particular way. Nothing has been named yet, we have no fix on place, or even space, and yet the character speaks out of a sense of what she wants. But it would be no less so if it started this way.

> 1: Excuse me.

He's still moving in the direction of his desire, toward what he wants, by breaking the silence, by starting things up. I don't have to move much past that utterance to see a sort of tension filling up the space. Where would you expect this to move from here? Direction is a natural part of dialogue. We expect to be led somewhere by the response. How will the other character deal with this? As the answer to this question becomes clearer, we often start to see the issue of distance, or separation, being defined. The tone of that response will set up speed. You might expect me to say that the tension I've set up demands that he reveal everything he wants in the first line. For now, let's have the second character work from a position of total neutrality.

1: Excuse me.
2: Yes?
1: Do you know the time?
2: No, I don't.
1: Do you have any sense of how long we've been here?
2: No.

That's probably as neutral as you're going to get. Still, speaker 2 is resisting. It's possible to read a certain distance into that exchange, an attitude that suggests speaker 2 isn't going to help speaker 1 in any way, shape or form. The brief responses lend an element of increased speed. Play it any way you want. Some element of tension is generally shaped by the act of speaking.

All good dialogue has direction. It's a mishmash of need and desire on the part of an individual character weighed against the tension inherent in the gathering of more than one person. Not convinced? Think there isn't always tension when people speak? "What about families?" you say. "What about people who love each other? There's not always tension there." Some of you are laughing at that already, because for many of us a family (love it as we may) is our greatest tissue of tensions. But I would remind you of my terms. This is not grand conflict here, not man versus nature; nor is it painful tension, nothing one could take care of with a little cup of tea and a foot rub. This is the stuff that fills the spaces between us, even when we don't recognize it. As a writer you have to learn to trust that it's there.

Go back to the conversation in the blank room. Try to make it as free of tension as possible. Would it look something like this?

1: Hi.

2: Hi.

1: How are you?

2: Fine. How are you?

1: Great. Nice day.

2: Really. Nice day.

Sounds hauntingly like those conversations we all have in elevators, or at a chance encounter, or in the hallways at school. Most people say they hate this kind of jabber, and in other places in the book, I've suggested, as I will again here, that there's no place for it in fiction. Sure people talk like this in the world, but that's why we must shape dialogue when we write. Good dialogue relies on a stronger tension than we see here. Good dialogue requires sharper word choice, more defined attitudes, more originality. As I said in chapter one, good dialogue should be something of an event unto itself.

But despite the apparent neutrality of the dialogue above, it is not without direction. Look at it again. Chart the direction using arrows if you want. Who starts the conversation? Speaker 1. ("Hi.") It's his energy that plays off the response too. Here, again, we might use the word "speed," or "pace." ("How are you?"). He's the one asking the questions. Speaker 2 is feeding off him. The arrows I'd draw would consistently be moving from 1 toward 2. That's one sort of tension, a sort of tensionless tension. Something that would take a long time to build up to the point where you might call it conflict, the point where 1 would want something from 2. It might end like this.

1: Fine then.

2: What do you mean?

1: Nothing.

2: Okay.

1: Fine.

2: I don't understand.

1: You wouldn't.

2: Are you angry?

1: No.

2: You seem angry. Have I done something wrong?

1: You just don't care. I'm sorry I ever talked to you.

That's an exaggeration, of course. And I have shaped things to my needs. That's what I believe you must do. But there's no question I have moved from the tension buried in the direction of an apparently neutral conversation and found one result. Could you nag out a neutral conversation for pages and pages, keeping it neutral the whole time? Your answer may be yes. Mine is no. That's the sort of thing we do in life. Jabber about sports, ask about the grandkids, exchange greetings. These are masks we wear. They don't last long before we start to reveal who we are. Put two people in one place, force them to listen to one another and soon they are telling stories or, more aptly for us I guess, telling stories in the act of telling. That is what the writer must believe.

Your challenge is to see the stories within the words of your character. Looking for speed, distance and direction and then manipulating these is a good place to start. If we accept that all good dialogue has these elements of tension, what is it that sets good dialogue apart from lifeless dialogue? Good dialogue rises out of the way a writer makes use of individual techniques, such as

- interruption
- silences
- echoing
- reversals
- shifts in tone and pace
- idiom
- detail

DIRECTED DIALOGUE

Let's look at an example that begins in a fairly "placeless" place, on the radio airwaves, on a radio talk show. This conversation opens Peter Abrahams' novel *The Fan*. This is one of those conversations we hear all the time. Read it once, then read it again, the second time looking for the tension that's buried in the direction of the speakers. I'll follow with a summary of the novel, and an overview of Gil, the main character, who is also the caller in this dialogue.

> "Who's next? Gil on the car phone. What's shakin', Gil?"
> Dead air.
> "Speak, Gil."

"Is this . . ."

"Go on."

"Hello?"

"You're on the JOC."

"Am I on?"

"Not for long, Gil, the way we're going. This is supposed to be entertainment."

Dead air.

"Got a question or a comment for us, Gil?"

"First-time caller."

"Fantabulous. What's on your mind?"

"I'm a little nervous."

"What's to be nervous? Just three million pairs of ears out there, hanging on your every word. What's the topic?"

"The Sox."

"I like the way you say that."

"How do I say it?"

"Like—what *else* could it be?"

Dead air.

"What about the Sox, Gil?"

"Just that I'm psyched, Bernie."

"Bernie's off today. This is Norm. Everybody gets psyched in the spring. That's a given in this game. Like ballpark mustard."

"This is different."

"How?"

Dead air.

"Gil?"

"I've been waiting a long time."

"For what?"

"This year."

"What's special about it?"

"It's their year."

"Why so tentative?"

"Tentative?"

"Just pulling your leg. The way you sound so sure. Like it's a lead-pipe cinch. The mark of the true-blue fan."

Dead air.

"Gil?"

"Yeah?"

"The Vegas odds are—what are they, Fred? Fred in the control room there, doing something repulsive with a pastrami on rye—ten to one on the Sox for the pennant, twenty, what is it, twenty-five to one on the whole shebang. Just to give us some perspective on this, Gil, what would you wager at those odds, if you were a wagering man?"

"Everything I owe."

"Owe? Hey. I like this guy. He's got a sense of humor after all. But, Gil—you're setting yourself up for a season of disillusion, my friend."

"Disillusion?"

"Yeah, like—"

"I know what *disillusion* means."

"Do you? Then you must—"

"They went down to the wire last year, didn't they?"

"Ancient history, Gil."

What is the charge that runs through this conversation? How and when do we begin to see the tensions of character revealed? The voice of the talk-show host is the active presence in the conversation, pressing against Gil's nervousness, against his stake in the team, against the public perception of the team, to shake him up, to force him into talking. His direction is clear, and, not surprisingly, Gil is not revealing enough for us to know many real facts about him. This is an openly antagonistic dialogue, one in which the movement of one character is an attempt to drive the tensions to the surface. The teasing, the cajoling, the chiding of the host are all a part of this. But so too is Gil's reluctance to speak, to reveal much about himself. The anonymity of the airwaves is a part of that, sure. But Gil's unwillingness or inability to reveal the tensions within him adds to the antagonism. Not surprising that what would follow is the dark story of Gil's obsessive relationship with a player and Gil's course of self-destruction. In the middle of the dialogue above, when Gil says, "I've been waiting a long time . . . [for] this year," it resonates, like all good dialogue, toward the story ahead, toward the year to come.

This is an example of directed dialogue, in which the writer is attempting to use dialogue as a means of setting up the tensions of the longer work. The particular tensions of this dialogue are reflective of issues that will come into play later. One character (in this case the

25

talk-show host) is used as foil for the other. At first it would appear that the host might be the center of this story, but as we read on, it becomes clear that Gil is the one with the story to tell. It's a fine example of a writer bringing tension directly to the surface through the dialogue itself.

The risk of directed dialogue is that it too often serves the needs of the writer first. It becomes a means of explanation, of exposition, and little more. What Abrahams does well is use the fast, staccato rhythm of the talk-show host to hedge the direction of the piece by employing some specific techniques.

- **Interruption.** When Gil cuts off the host with, "I know what disillusion means," this is another moment where his story is foreshadowed.
- **Silences.** Represented here as "Dead air."
- **Echoing.** "Everything I owe" followed by "Owe? . . ." One speaker often picks up or repeats the last word of the previous speaker.
- **Reversals.** The host moves from sarcasm ("Fantabulous") to challenging ("What's special about it?") to chiding ("Ancient history, Gil.").
- **Shifts in pace.** This is an excellent example of a dialogue that works well without dialogue tags.
- **Shifts in tone.** The dialogue lurches forward when it moves from the host's glib line about "ballpark mustard" to Gil's grim response: "This is different."
- **Convincing use of idiom.** "You're on the JOC."
- **Strong details.** The references to the Sox, ballpark mustard, etc.

These elements hold this dialogue, and the others like it in the book, together, allowing it to work for the writer to advance plot and to serve as a convincing reflection of Gil's world. That's the best effect of directed dialogue.

INTERPOLATED DIALOGUE

The artificial part of directed dialogue is that it requires two characters to be "stuck" in one place long enough for them to open up their lives to the reader through conversation. How many conversations have you had in which all your hopes and fears are revealed, at least in part, within a few exchanges? Odds are not many. Those moments do come, but most often the writer must choose ways to isolate specific moments of dialogues or specific directions within these dialogues to reveal the heart of the character. Often this requires interpolating the dialogue with narrative. Interpolating a dialogue allows the narrative to interrupt and interpret the dialogue. Often a single line of dialogue is interpolated into a far larger moment in the scope of the story than it is in the lives of the characters themselves. Take a simple, one-word response like "Sure." Lines like this pass our way again and again in dialogue, but think for a moment about ways to make this word tie in to the life of a character in some meaningful way. Our character may be saying it unwillingly and with a sense of resignation. To interpolate a moment like this, the narrative might step in, interrupting the dialogue on the page, to unwind the character's life in some way, perhaps touching on all the other times she'd simply given in like that. While this may sound intimidating, it ought to be the stuff writers rub their hands over, as it allows for direct connection from the external world of event to the internal world of the character.

In Anton Chekhov's great story "The Lady With the Pet Dog," a moment of casual conversation becomes a looking glass into a character's soul. The story centers on Dmitry Dmitrovich, a Muscovite in late nineteenth-century Russia. His public life, and married life, leaves him unsatisfied and melancholy and, on vacation in Yalta, he meets a woman with whom he begins an affair. He is rejuvenated by the relationship, but as it would be destructive to both his life and the woman's, he must keep it a secret. His life is split in two, and while he discovers his humanity in his new love, he is trapped by the world in which he lives. At one point, he leaves a restaurant and feels the urge to share his secret. Read the passage below and notice how little is actually spoken but how much is revealed in the words and reactions of the characters. This interpolated dialogue, brief as it is, has a direction too. Its effect, however, is made clear through the narrative that precedes and follows it.

> Already he was tormented by a strong desire to share his memories with someone. But, in his home it was impossible to talk of his love, and he had no one to talk to outside; certainly he could not confide in his tenants or in anyone at the bank. And what was there to talk about? He hadn't loved then, had he? Had there been anything beautiful, poetical, edifying or simply

interesting in his relations with Anna Sergeyevna? And he was forced to talk vaguely of love, of women, and no one guessed what he meant; only his wife would twitch her black eyebrows and say, "The part of the philanderer does not suit you at all, Dmitry."

One evening, coming out of the physician's club with an official with whom he had been playing cards, he could not resist saying:

"If you only knew what a fascinating woman I became acquainted with at Yalta!"

The official got into his sledge and was driving away, but turned suddenly and shouted:

"Dmitry Dmitrovich!"

"What is it?"

"You were right this evening: the sturgeon was a bit high."

These words, so commonplace, for some reason moved Gurov to indignation, and struck him as degrading and unclean. What savage manner, what mugs! What stupid nights, what dull humdrum days! Frenzied gambling, gluttony, drunkenness, continual talk always about the same things! Futile pursuits and conversations always about the same topics take up the better part of one's time, the better part of one's strength, and in the end there is left a life clipped and wingless, an absurd mess, and there is no escaping or getting away from it—just as though one were in a prison.

Although Peter Abrahams would surely cringe at the comparison to a master like Chekhov, it's important to note ways in which this dialogue is completely different from the one cited from *The Fan*. This passage acts as one of the story's moments of clarity, an epiphany in which the character sees his life stripped to its most brutal essence. Yet, the dialogue itself is short and the explicit meaning of what is said would not appear to apply to the protagonist's life in any larger sense. It is a moment that, without the accompanying narrative, might appear to be just another moment of daily jabber. But this brief exchange, in which Dmitry's associate tells him the fish was "high," meaning a bit spoiled, just as Dmitry is about to reveal his heart, represents something far larger, and Chekhov attaches a lyric piece of narrative exposition to the dialogue directly. Like the passage before it, this dialogue reveals, but the interruption and interpretation of the narrative drives home the point of what is *not* said, rather than what is said. This is where the interpolation comes in. The dialogue is realistic; the narrative is expository and interpretive. The two are clearly attached, without apology, by the writer. It's not about filling silences so much as filling the gaps left by our words, the gaps between us.

Interpolation is part of the way we tell stories to one another. It is part of the internal texture of a character. Picture yourself telling someone about an argument you had.

> *"Then I said, 'No, I won't have it ready. Not when you want it.'*
> That's what I told him. My life is a mess. I'm behind in everything, the reports pile up faster than I can get them out and I just hate the new payroll system. I hold everything in, too. I mean I really bury it. I hate it all. I look at everything on my desk and I just want to start fresh."

The sentence in italics represents what was literally said; what follows is interpretation for the intended audience. Maybe you recognize interpolation now. Within the frame of a story, it is tempting to allow the flow of dialogue to take over your pace and treatment of scene. Once again, it is important to think about the way we tell jokes, stories, related memories. Stating what literally happened is often less important than the interpretation of those events. Hitting the dialogue right is a matter of seeing where the tension is in the character's life.

Still, don't overexplain. Go back to real life. Some writers do this sort of interpreting incessantly. Don't they wear you out? Let that serve as your warning. Don't fall into a pattern of interrupting and interpreting every snatch of dialogue. Interpolated dialogue is difficult, and when poorly done can sink your work. Use this tool wisely. A good rule is if you find yourself explaining only for the reader's benefit, then stop. If you are discovering things for yourself, press on.

MISDIRECTED DIALOGUE

What about dialogue where the movement seems random? People don't answer one another. Subjects change without warning. Characters respond to stray thoughts and show no interest in a progression of tensions. Call this type of dialogue misdirected. Misdirected dialogue brings in so many strands of existence that its direction resists diagnosis. It appears to operate without direction, in open defiance of the whole notion. It sounds, quite often, more like real conversations.

Lorrie Moore uses this approach in the following scene from her novel *Who Will Run the Frog Hospital?* Here the narrator and her husband are lying in bed talking. The novel takes place in Paris, where the narrator has come to sort out her life and where her husband has an academic engagement. Read the dialogue below and look for all the different directions presented; the first line appears rather direct, but within moments, the two are speaking in metaphors.

> "I'm not really looking forward to going home," I say now.
> "Really?"
> "I feel disconnected these days, in the house, in town. The neighbors say, 'Hello, how are you?' and sometimes I say, 'Oh, I'm feeling a little empty today. How about you?' "
> "You should get a puppy," he says sleepily.
> "A puppy?"
> "Yeah. It's not like the cat. A puppy you can take for walks around the neighborhood, and people will stop and smile and say, 'Ooooh, look—what's wrong with your puppy?' "
> "What is wrong with my puppy?"
> "Worms, I think. I don't know. You should have taken him to the vet's weeks ago."
> "You're so mean."
> "I'm sorry I'm not what you bargained for," Daniel murmurs.
> I stop and think about this. "Well, I'm not what you bargained for, either, so we're even."
> "No," he says faintly, "you are. You're what I bargained for."
> But then he has fallen over the cliff of sleep and is snoring, his adenoids a kind of engine in his face, a motorized unit, a security system like a white flag going up.

The movement here works in waves. The tension between the two characters is high. Just when one character is being direct, the other evades and dances away. The lack of direct response is a sign of intimacy, ironically. There is a code to their language which makes the exchange, with its blend of quiet revelation and gentle chiding, something recognizable and at the same time foreign. Such is the case with misdirected dialogue.

Misdirected dialogue is the type of dialogue that most naturally takes advantage of the rhythms and cadences of language I have been encouraging you to look for. It relies on the fact that life does not always shape itself to the needs of plot, and it turns the mirror on the clamor of voices that surround us, on the natural tendency to leave tensions hanging, rather than march toward resolution. This sort of dialogue sounds more natural and allows tension to build more slowly than in dialogue that's shaped with a heavy sense of direction. It's more surprising, more challenging, and sounds more like the sort of stuff we hear in the world around us. Misdirection is a tool for surprise to be sure, but it brings complexity and ambiguity to our conception of the world within our fiction. Listen for it in the world around you. Use it in the fiction you craft. Its elements include:

- changing the subject
- directing the dialogue "offstage"
- answering questions with answers that aren't quite answers but sound like them
- allowing characters to speak to themselves, for themselves
- carrying on more than one conversation at the same time

Crafting Misdirection

Start with three people in a restaurant. Rather than starting with a tension, begin by hearing them speak. You've had lots of practice with this by now. Push them to reveal their tensions. This is the key to creating misdirected dialogue. Allow them to speak in random order, but do not force it.

1: I need a beer. Could I have a beer?
2: I saw Marnie today.
1: Beer, please.
3: Where did you see her?
1: You know. By the fire station.
3: No kidding.
1: Her hair has grown.
3: I would imagine. How do you know?
1: I'm not blind.

2: Are you eating?

3: Did you see her too?

1: You see her everywhere. She's like That Girl! Those hats!

2: I'm eating. I'm starving.

3: I'm just asking.

1: I saw her last week. As a matter of fact I remarked on her hair.

2: The TV show?

3: You talked to her?

2: Who?

1: Marnie.

3: Marnie.

2: You're kidding. I just saw her today myself.

Not brilliant. But it does follow the rules I suggested. What occurs is that the dialogue moves in different directions as each character starts to respond to the others. Notice the techniques: changing the subject (when speaker 1 brings up the hair); part of it is directing the dialogue "offstage" (when speaker 1 calls for beer); part of it is answering questions with answers that aren't quite answers but sound like them ("How do you know?" followed by "I'm not blind."); another part is allowing characters to speak to themselves, for themselves ("I'm eating. I'm starving."); part of it involves carrying on more than one conversation at the same time.

If you found the conversation difficult to follow, that probably had much to do with the fact that I gave the characters no names, that I attached scenic details and I paced the exchanges to be quick and somewhat sharp. There is, however, a literal direction to this, one that can be better imagined by rewriting the dialogue in columns.

(1)	(2)	(3)
I need a beer. Could I have a beer?		
	I saw Marnie today.	
Beer, please.		
		Where did you see her?
You know. By the fire station.		

(1)	(2)	(3)
		No kidding.
Her hair has grown.		
		I would imagine. How do you know?
I'm not blind.		
	Are you eating?	
		Did you see her too?
You see her everywhere. She's like That Girl! Those hats!		
	I'm eating. I'm starving.	
		I'm just asking.
I saw her last week. As a matter of fact I remarked on her hair.		
	The TV show?	
		You talked to her?
	Who?	
Marnie.		
		Marnie.
	You're kidding. I just saw her today myself.	

Draw arrows from one line to the line that evoked that response and you'll start to see how the patterning works here. Still, it's no parlor trick. Misdirected dialogue often balances tensions against one another in the most explicit fashion. Not for one minute do more voices mean a less diffuse tension. Indeed more voices mean more characters, more characters mean more needs. The key with misdirection is to recognize that it's easy to confuse the reader with evasion and patterning, but you do more to capture a reader when she starts to recognize these unnamable patterns even as the characters continue to speak.

MODULATED DIALOGUE
A fourth type of dialogue, modulated dialogue, uses narrative commentary and scenic detail to extend the complexity of expression.

Here the movement is not from one character to another (as in directed dialogue) nor into the life of one character in particular (as in interpolated dialogue). The movement is not particularly between characters either (as in misdirected dialogue). In modulated dialogue, each piece of dialogue becomes a point of entry for the writer to drift toward other details. Memory can be modulated into a dialogue easily and clearly. A character's words call up a forgotten moment, a flashback ensues and at its close, the dialogue begins again. The narrator can comment openly on the "meaning" of the words passing before us on the page.

If all of that sounds pretty bloodless and technical, keep in mind that when memory and place work their way into your dialogues to their fullest measure, your fiction is doing its finest, truest work. You can use modulated dialogue as a means of exploring the tensions more explicitly, of complicating the present, or for advancing the current plot line with a key flashback.

Rich in Love, by Josephine Humphreys, is a novel that explores many of these same connections through the voice and consciousness of a sixteen-year-old narrator named Lucille Odom, who witnesses the breakup of her parents' marriage and the dissolution of their family with a mixture of fear, wisdom and desire. Many of the dialogues in this book stretch over pages and are interrupted by memory, place and revelation. A good modulated dialogue takes place when she goes to lunch with her erstwhile boyfriend, Wayne Frobiness and his father, who puts Wayne on the spot about money.

> "... and I want you to guess how much I have to pay for liability insurance. Guess."
>
> "I couldn't begin to."
>
> "No, just take a wild guess. What do you think I have to cough up?"
>
> "I don't know." Wayne was stubborn. I knew he wouldn't guess.
>
> "Take a guess, son," Dr. Frobiness insisted.
>
> "A million dollars," I said.
>
> "Heh, no, little lady, not quite that much. No, I'm ponying up *twenty-one thousand* dollars a year for insurance." He pronounced the first syllable of "thousand" with a wide open mouth, and made his eyes big.

"Holy smoke," I said, to be polite. In truth, I thought that was a pretty good bargain. Suppose he botched a liposuction or misaligned an implant? If I were the insurance company, I would not have insured Dr. Frobiness for any amount.

He went on to say that some fathers, himself and Ronald Reagan included, had a lot at stake in the careers of their sons. It wasn't as if the sons of such fathers were free agents. "My heart aches for the President," he said.

"Excuse me," I said. I wanted seconds before they wheeled the roast beef away. It was already three o'clock, and the steamboat round was carved down the middle like a saddle. The waiter in charge of slicing meat was standing over by the aquarium with two other waiters. I waited politely by the meat, plate in hand, but they were engaged in an argument, and a partially melted seahorse made of ice stood between me and them. They didn't notice me. One said, "Maître d' said, get that mother *out*." Another said, "Get him out how?" "I don't know, but get him out." "Shit, man, I ain't reaching my hand in there. It's crabs in there." "He ain't dead yet anyhow." "Sure he is." "Naw, he ain't. His gills is opening and closing, that's his breathing." "Any fish that is upside down is dead in my book." "Said get him out fast before a member sees him." "Get him out, James." "Go for it, James." "All *right, James.*"

There are two types of modulation going on here. The first occurs when the narrator allows the dialogue to fall away and replaces it with the speculation about Dr. Frobiness. In the "present" of our narration, time is passing, yet the dialogue, merely related here, does not reflect that. A similar sort of modulation occurs when Lucille stands and moves to the carving table. In this instance, place, including the fine example of an untagged dialogue (lines that appear without "he said" or specific indication of speaker), takes over, and expands. When the girl returns to the table moments later, more than a page and a half of description has risen to fill up the moments. The dialogue between father and son, to which our narrator is primarily a witness, marches on after the digression, and nothing is lost for the reader in terms of time of understanding.

Writing Dialogue and the exercises within it press you toward modulation. I believe it is the bread and butter of good fiction. A well-modulated dialogue captures scene, tension and an element of the background consciousness in the story and allows the story to rise above the constraints of our artless lives. It allows for the insinuation of beauty and irony. Those things that make a dialogue the backbone of a scene. It is a chance for the narrative consciousness to work in tension with the character's consciousness. Here, unlike interpolated dialogue, the emphasis is not on interpretation but on the collision of details and the art that rises out of it.

THE DANGER OF CLASSIFYING

The danger here is that by defining and classifying these types of dialogue, I have tempted you to think about them as distinctly separate forms of writing, as if one day you will be working with interpolation whereas the next should be saved for directed dialogue only. These forms are not mutually exclusive. When a dialogue is "directed" by a particular need or emotion, that does not mean that scene has to disappear, that memory cannot be modulated into it or that evasion and misdirection cannot be used. Classifications are for biologists, God bless them. Just be aware that dialogue operates around energy and direction. As you write, tune in to the elements. Be aware of the pitfalls of explaining too much and of not explaining at all. Tread a line between too much scene and too little, between too few voices and too many. But *know* the line first.

The key is to read self-consciously, to watch what the writer is doing. Accept nothing as a pure reflection of "real life," as you know by now that dialogue is always shaped. As you read, draw arrows, make charts, watch for patterning. Don't feel the need to ape these patterns straight out, but don't be afraid to either. Soon they will become your signature, as you layer and modulate the voices you create and the world they inhabit in your own distinctive fashion.

EXERCISES

1. Using the example from the chapter as a model, write a dialogue between three or more people *in columns*. Or find an existing dialogue, and chart it in that fashion. Pause after one page. Assess the flow and direction of the dialogue. At what points is the direction too predictable? Mark these moments, then begin again. This time, let no two characters speak back and forth more than once. Incorporate more

voices. Add a column. Have one character speak to someone we can't see. Allow them to speak to one another by interrupting. Reconsider and vary the length of these lines. Now write the dialogue in a "straight fashion," modulating scene and memory as appropriate. In what ways is the dialogue "misdirected" and what do these movements reveal?

2. Try writing the same dialogue in the four different styles mentioned in this chapter: directed, interpolated, misdirected and modulated. Choose one that's long enough to provide plenty of material and clearly set within the context of a larger story.

Some watchwords:

Directed dialogue: Be sure to strip away as much of the outside world as possible. Place the tension on the surface. Allow the words of the characters to bear the weight of moving the plot and tension of the scene. In directed dialogue, emotion is often quite near the surface. Keep description to a minimum.

Interpolated dialogue: Take a line or two from the dialogue you create and allow the narrative to subsume the rest of the conversation. Interpolative dialogue is about interpreting. Pull the tensions into an interpretation of the significance of the given line. The line that triggers the moment of realization can be small, but the realization should be grand. Shoot out of the moment toward the heart and soul of the character.

Misdirected dialogue: Here remember the list of techniques I gave you. Try them out. They include

- changing the subject
- directing the dialogue "offstage"
- answering questions with answers that aren't quite answers but sound like them
- allowing characters to speak to themselves, for themselves
- carrying on more than one conversation at the same time

Pattern the dialogue so answers come late, or don't come at all. Allow characters to speak suddenly, to interrupt, to evade. Pull in details to jar the scene, rather than to reinforce the theme at play. Allow many people to speak up, in many ways.

Modulated dialogue: Pull out all the stops. Force scene or memory to become a new and surprising part of the existing dialogue. Look around! Look back! Allow each line of dialogue to become a window into some other element of the story: Place. Character. Tension. Allow your narration to comment on what is being said and why.

If, when starting either of these exercises, you are stuck for an idea for a scenario, you might try one of these:

Two couples on a hotel balcony in Cairo, at night, drinks in hand

Two men ice fishing

Two women painting an old church pew

Three children who discover a shoe box full of human teeth

THREE

DIALOGUE AND CHARACTER

The way people speak defines who they are. Think of the people you know. Everyone knows people who are uncomfortable in a room with even one stranger in it. They clam up, setting their faces calmly and firmly against the unfamiliar circumstances. Or people babble, despite their best intentions, trying to poke in something to say at every turn, keeping the conversation under their control, where the unfamiliar person is kept at a distance. Two rhythms, one circumstance, two entirely different characters.

Run with me on this. With the first character, the silent one, don't you automatically get your own sense of the character details? Gender? Clothes? Position in the room? All that and more, without a word. The same probably holds true about the babbler. She might laugh at her own jokes, or repeat herself, or interrupt repeatedly. We begin to see who she is without hearing anything particular from her.

Dialogue feeds through, and grows from, character. Voice, as an element of dialogue, is a product of the writer's understanding of an individual character.

PARTICULARS OF CHARACTER

There is a lot of talk in fiction writing about finding your voice. It is, in most senses, a search every writer undertakes, finding out what she wants to say by discovering *how* she should say it. It is an issue of craft, a question of talent, work habit and common sense. But it is important to recognize that finding your voice as a writer is an issue of narrative control rather than of shaping the voice of your characters.

There's a difference between the voice of your work and the voices you employ within it. You have to be able to recognize this difference and take advantage of it.

Undoubtedly, there are times when a single character will want to tell a story, be it long or short, and that character's voice will become the vehicle for the story, if not its whole reason for being. That's narrative voice. But each character within a story speaks with his own voice as much as, if not more than, in the voice of the writer. Ironically, your job as a writer is often a matter of separating yourself from your own voice, of tuning into the particulars of character and of growing the voice within it.

There are certain obvious factors. Age, for instance. Think of all the children you know. Pause at the municipal pool. Does the sunburnt, jubilant five-year-old drum the same conversational rhythms as the sullen fifteen-year-old lifeguard? Of course not. Aren't the two so far apart in circumstance, experience, vocabulary and even knowledge of the world as to make a comparison pointless? I start with children here because the differences between ages are so readily apparent. Age separates and defines.

Compare in your mind's eye—or in your spiral notebook, should you be traveling—that sunburnt five-year-old at your local pool in, say, Metropolis, Illinois, to the five-year-old in Dade County, Florida. The similarities may shine brightest at first, but with a little listening, you'll start to hear the edges of the words and sentences reveal the particulars of each kid's life. You have to listen for particulars like pace, tone and word choice. Not surprisingly, I think it helps to record this stuff in your spiral to look at the way each kid's words fall together. Soon it's more than an age you see. It's the circumstance; it's a family; it's the local dialect; it's the way these kids are talked to and the places where they are heard.

DICTION AND DIALECT

Where I live now, in western Indiana, people tend to drop the "to be" verb from their sentences when they speak. When looking at a dirty rug, they say, "That needs washed," rather than, "That needs to be washed." Frankly, it's a pretty solid economy of language that allows this, but the habit does grate on the ear at the outset. When I first moved here, I couldn't quite pick up on this difference. I put down the local dialect to a matter of twang and accent. Only when I started writing about my life in Indiana did I realize that words were missing, and only when I started to give voice to characters who lived here did I start to hear and—once on the page—*see* the differences of the rhythms of their language. The spiral notebook comes into play again. Record.

My mother looks at the dirty rug and says, "That is filthy. It ought to be cleaned." My neighbor says, "That needs washed." My cousin from Long Island: "That's gotta be cleaned." A librarian in Maine: "That needs a washing." My brother looks at the dirty rug and says, "Nice. Sandblast that thing." Did I show these people the rug? Of course not. I listened to them.

When I wrote those responses, I tried to think of these people as characters. I gave them a chance to speak. If I've listened hard enough, the subtle differences in diction and syntax should reveal themselves. Again, it's often a matter of pace. My brother tends to punch his words out in quick bursts; his diction tends to be a reflection of attitude. My neighbor, a former fireman, is a taciturn, commonsense fellow. The fewer words the better. My mother tends toward precision, exactness. Do I think these things consciously, as I am letting each character "speak"? Not at all. But I do try to call up certain resonances of each person's voice. I do try to hear each one, literally. If you can't hear your characters speak, then what they say most often ought not be said. That doesn't mean they can't be in the mix. It might mean that they don't have to speak. My father, for instance, would just look at the dirty rug and shake his head at the fact that I had let it get so bad. That, too, is a sort of dialogue exchange.

The differences in the above responses are mostly a matter of diction, or word choice, and syntax, or word order. Diction is the key element in the initial shaping of a character's voice. Forget the sound of his voice for a minute. Forget accent. Forget pace. Think word choice.

Whether we do it sloppily or beautifully, speaking is one of our primary skills as human beings. Yet when we do speak, we hardly encounter the choices we are making. Rarely do we think of our words as a matter of choice. Consider how difficult it can be for some to write and deliver a speech. Each word read aloud in that circumstance is a reminder of the choices the writer/speaker made. Word choice becomes an issue.

Yet when you fall into a conversation with a woman while waiting for a bus, you don't take a deep breath and think, *Geez, now I have to think of some words. I have to choose what I'm going to say. Perhaps I'll start with a present participle.* You speak. The words well out of you. You are a human being. You are an animal of language.

In the above example, where people look at the dirty rug, each response is different enough from the other that the reader can begin to hear the same voices the writer is hearing. Notice that there is not a lot of work going on with accent and tone. You can create strong dialogue by concentrating on word choice. Those other factors—the way you say it, your accent, your use of idiom and dialect—are all secondary to word choice. When crafting dialogue, diction rules.

Good diction lends precision. When chosen correctly, a character's diction can show us who she is, what she knows. John Casey's wonderful novel *Spartina*, the story of Dick Pierce, a struggling Rhode Island Fisherman, is a book in which you can see the diction associated with a job as ancient and complicated as fishing. At first, the terminology seems obtuse to someone who's never lived near the water, but soon the reader sees the precise way the characters speak of the job at hand as a sort of natural shorthand. In one scene, Dick is forced to leave an inexperienced woman in a smaller boat following a marlin already hooked, as he sets out to follow a second marlin. After catching the fish, he radios a plane, which they have been using to watch for large fish from above. Read the scene that ensues and notice how much the particular word choice, the idioms of the job, define the understanding these men have of the job. Mark the words you are unfamiliar with in this context.

> Parker raised the plane, which they could see way back where they'd come from.
>
> The pilot said the first fish seemed to be still going, still fast to the keg, the dory tagging along.
>
> Dick said, "Maybe we should've took our chances, just let the spotter find the keg."
>
> "The plane can't haul the fish," Parker said. "Maybe she'll scare off the sharks."

Not terribly confusing, but if you didn't understand that the fish had been "kegged," harpooned to a line attached to a metal keg, you'd be at a loss. And if you didn't know that a "dory" was a small boat and that the "spotter" was the plane, you'd be struggling too. You might recognize the idiomatic use of the word "fast" in "fast to the keg" as meaning "holding" or "attached." I could have explained all that before you read the selection, but that would be supplanting the use of precise diction and appropriate idiom. These words and expressions are appropriate because they are appropriate to this world.

Moreover they are appropriate to these people. It's no great secret that all of us use language in a fashion forged from some conglomerate of social forces. In the example from *Spartina*, we see the edges of a regional dialect in this line: "Maybe we should've took our chances, just let the spotter find the keg."

The line has grammatical problems and missing words. We'll get to dialect soon, but notice how Casey is doing it. A subtle mix of idiom, precise choices of diction and minor variations in syntax (word placement).

In Frederick Busch's strange and wonderful story "Dog Song," the protagonist, a judge, wakes up in a hospital room after having driven his car into a telephone pole. Each time he wakes, he is faced with a memory that reveals more and more of his complex and painful life to him. He often wakes to his own pain and to the presence of unfamiliar people—nurses, doctors, other patients—who appear in the story as disembodied voices. Here's one such scene. Notice how the small variations in the order of this stranger's words help us to draw a picture of him.

> He heard his breath shudder now, in the salmon-colored room, mostly shadows and walnut veneers. Then he heard a man say, "You wanna nurse?"
>
> "Who?"
>
> "It's me. You can't turn, huh? Listen, Your Honor, it's such a pain in the ass as well as the armpit, the crutches, I'm gonna stay flat for a while. I'll visit you later on, you can look at me and remember. I'm the guy said hello the other time."
>
> "You're in here with me?"
>
> "Yeah. Ain't it an insult? You a judge and everything. Like the doctor said, it's real crowded."

"This is *too* crowded."

"Well, listen, don't go extending any special treatment to me, Your Honor. Just pretend I'm a piece of dog shit. You'll feel better if you don't strain for the little courtesies and all. Your wife's a very attractive woman, if I may say so. Hell of a temper, though."

In this case, the character comes to life through his words alone, since the protagonist can't see him. Read the voice aloud. Once you've read it through, gauge for yourself: What sort of man is the judge's roommate? What can you tell from his tone? Is he threatening in some fashion? Insincere? Is he a poor man? A dangerous man? If he had used standard English, would we have lost some sense of who he is?

The original line from *Spartina*, which appears previously, is this.

Maybe we should've took our chances, just let the spotter find the keg.

Translate it so it reads grammatically, and it loses some authenticity.

Maybe we should have taken our chances and just let the spotter plane find the keg.

Translated even further to make the situation crystal clear to the reader, we begin to see why we need to hear the voices through variations in diction and syntax.

Perhaps we should have risked losing the first fish. We could have let the spotter follow the keg.

Here I've created dialogue that clarifies the dilemma they are in, but it does nothing to show who they are. This is an example of dialogue serving the needs of the story rather than the realities of the characters. The words people choose (diction) and the way they use them (syntax) can do much to show us who they are. We do not have to reinvent language to show peculiarities of a dialect. We can and should make use of the language as we know it. That is the key to varying diction and syntax. Reinventing them is poetry. Using them accurately and convincingly is a particularly important key to writing strong dialogue.

THE QUESTION OF DIALECT

Most people assume that dialect has to be a part of dialogue. My answer is that it can be, and in certain circumstances it ought to be, but *the writer must never feel compelled to duplicate dialects simply for the sake of "authenticity."* The writer who thinks she is writing dialect because she is clipping the ends off of words and stretching out others is often taking delight more in her own experimentation that in any real sense of story. She may be shooting for a folksy charm or for a root authenticity, but most often she fails miserably. Try all you want to make the words unrecognizable—misspell them, cut them in half, throw in a fistful of apostrophes, sound out every groan the character makes—the truth is, they are still words you're dealing with. Consider this example. Two grandmothers sit on a porch in Tennessee; one of them is trying to convince the other to go into town to get a pie from the grocery store to serve at dinner the next day.

> "Sho' 'nuff smo time leff fo you to git on downtown fo' 'nother pan dat pie."
> "Ain't but a-our o' two leff in the day. Dat walk take lease three hours, dere and back."
> "But 'choo know dey love dat pie. Ah shore-ly do. You too. Ah love to serve that pie at a good suppa. Please git on."
> "Ah had a car, Ah'd go. Aint no car workin' in walkin distance tis whole place. Ah know you want dat pie. Ah know you do. Ah set out, maybe to barra Kip's hahrse and buggy."
> "Ah hope so, light's afailin."

This is incredibly bad. The story is okay (we'll get to that). But the language is absurdly disguised behind the pretense of dialect. To be sure, it is an exaggeration. But each choice made by the writer—a misspelling here, an apostrophe there—is a little piece of what most people consider to be the essence of writing dialect. That is, it shoots for the sound of the words rather than the words themselves. In this case, it is difficult to read, complicated to decipher and once done, it's hard for the reader to get a sense of anything outside of the basic question set up by the exposition that preceded it.

But wait. Perhaps you *can* read it, and while maybe you can't understand every detail, you like it. That's right, you think, that's the way they talk in the South! You *like* reading dialogue aloud, sounding words out for their music. I give you high marks for liking the music of language, but if you like this kind of writing, buy yourself a French horn and try to blow Shakespeare through it. You're sure to get a clearer use of language than that garbage. While you're at it, you might coat-check your preconceptions on human beings in the southern half of the United States because no matter how poor, how ignorant, how little traveled people in Tennessee might be (or in the Bronx for that matter), they use language when they speak, and language is more than jamming a washcloth in the mouth of the speaker to get at the "sound." Don't be so high-minded as to assume you know a dialect because you've seen some reruns of *The Dukes of Hazzard* and you own a copy of *As I Lay Dying*. All language has a logic; all language has dignity. It's words as much as sounds.

If you are from Tennessee, right now you are (rightly) about to throw this book across the room, because every attempt at tonality in that exchange is slightly off, every instance of localized syntax is forced and there are, you can surely see, inconsistencies of dialect even within the sentences these people speak. Go ahead, throw it. But only if you're from Tennessee. Then pick it back up because we're about to translate that passage and fix it.

The first thing to do with any piece of dialogue is figure out the story. Read that crummy one about the pie again. Don't look for the entire story, but more simply for the story of this dialogue. In a case like this, with bad dialogue, we're translating more than anything else. Still, not surprisingly, you should begin with character. What does each person want? Determining this should allow you some sense of pace and rhythm. Examine tension next. What is holding these people together or keeping them apart? Then I'd look at setting. What's brought them to the same place? Where are they?

As we saw in chapter two, when discussing tension, these are good diagnostic questions for nearly any dialogue. The answers to them show us what dialogue should do in the broadest sense:

- bring characters and conflict into focus
- be driven by the needs of the characters, more than by the needs of the story
- locate us, give us a sense of where we are, who we are listening to

Let's apply these questions to the dialogue involving the women and the pie.

- **What do they want?** The women seem to want pie. But one woman wants, or needs (we can't be sure), the other woman to go get the pie. It appears someone is coming to visit them ("dey" love it; there is mention of a "good suppa"; there's anxiety about getting the pie before night falls).

- **What's holding them together?** It would appear they depend on each other somehow. One woman is urging the other to do something for the both of them. It would appear that the issues of the larger story might come out of this question.

- **Where are they?** Somewhere isolated (as the walk for the pie is over three hours), as they don't seem to have any neighbors with cars who could help them.

When a story is choked by dialect, the way this little dialogue is, you have to work your way back to story through language. The writer of this sort of dialogue would probably say you have to read it aloud to understand it. When you do that, it becomes clear that "Ah" equals "I" and "dat" is "that." This is a good illustration of relying too heavily on dialect. Right now you are probably saying words like "Ah" out loud. To some of them, this reads like the sound the doctor asks you to make before he swabs your tonsils for strep; for other readers, it is more nasal, sounding like a grunt made in midstride of an argument ("Ah . . . yeah. That's true, but . . . ah . . . I have another point to make on that matter."). The word has become a sound. A word created to mimic sound has to be an absolute success in terms of its music. There are entire novels where this happens (Alice Walker's *The Color Purple* comes to mind), but in these books, the entire thread of the novel teaches the reader the language of these sounds. We can't presume to do the same within the short dialogue we're discussing, but tweaking just a little bit for tension and otherwise just translating the dialogue, it looks something like this.

> *Sho' 'nuff smo time leff fo you to git on downtown fo' 'nother pan dat pie.* "There's still time enough for you to get downtown for another pan of that pie."

Ain't but a-our o' two leff in the day. Dat walk take lease three hours, dere and back. "Ain't but an hour left in the day. That walk would take at least three hours, there and back."

But 'choo know dey love dat pie. Ah shore-ly do. You too. Ah love to serve that pie at a good suppa. Please git on. "Please get on. You know they love that pie. I surely do. You do too. At a good supper, I love to serve that pie. Please."

Ah had a car, Ah'd go. Ain't no car workin' in walkin distance tis whole place. Ah know you want dat pie. Ah know you do. Ah set out, maybe to barra Kip's hahrse and buggy. "If I had a car, I'd go. Ain't no working car even in walking distance. Shoot. I know you want that pie. I know it. Maybe I'll set out to borrow Kip's horse and buggy."

Ah hope so, light's afailin. "I hope so. The light's failing."

The language here contains plenty of dialect. But now the dialect is basically confined to word choice and syntax rather than spelling and misspelling. The machinations of dialect no longer keep us from meaning; rather they lead us to it. The accent is there for the reader, but it doesn't overwhelm the scene. Nor should it, ever.

Dialect That Works

There are writers crafting excellent dialect out there: Gloria Naylor, Junot Díaz, Sherman Alexie, Alice Walker, the poet June Jordan, Susan Straight, Sapphire, Toni Morrison, Amy Tan, Gus Lee, Earl Lovelace, among others. Then there are the champions of the ages. William Faulkner comes to mind immediately. What works beautifully in Faulkner's dialect is that it is so heavily modulated with the narrative it becomes a sort of true music. The sounds of the characters' language tears through the narrative consciousness of the novel. It is a part of the sound of the whole novel, the whole experience of reading a Faulkner story, the experience of Faulkner's world. Consider this passage from *The Bear*. Watch how the narrative shifts fluidly from the one dialect to the other and then into the movement of the narration. In this scene, seven strangers wander in to join in Major De Spain's epic hunt for the bear.

They were swampers: gaunt, malaria-ridden men appearing from nowhere, who ran trap-lines for coons or perhaps farmed little patches of cotton and corn along the edge of the bottom, in clothes but little better than Sam Father's and nowhere near as good as Tennie Jim's, with worn shotguns and rifles, already squatting patiently in the cold drizzle in the side yard when the day broke. They had a spokesman. . . . "Mawnin, Major. We heerd you was aimin to put that ere blue dawg on that old two-toed bear this mawnin. We figgered we'd come up and watch, if you don't mind. We won't do no shooting, lessen he runs over us."

"You are welcome," Major De Spain said. "You are welcome to shoot. He's more your bear than ours."

"I reckon that ain't no lie. I done fed him enough cawn to have a sheer in him. Not to mention a shoat three year sago."

"I reckon I got a sheer too," another said. "Only it ain't in the bear." Major De Spain looked at him. He was chewing tobacco. He spat. "It was a heifer calf. Nice un too. Last year. When I finally found her, I reckon she looked about like that colt of yourn last June."

"Oh," said Major De Spain. "Be welcome. If you see game in front of my dogs shoot it."

The center of this scene is the meeting of these men and the history they share. The scene does not revolve around Faulkner's use of dialect. It is merely an element within the scene. The dialect is governed by a logic and consistency, demonstrated here and throughout the novel. It is difficult to read, but it ebbs and flows through the momentum of the narrative, never obscuring meaning.

Many exciting contemporary writers try to bring dialect to the center of their work. James Kelman, a Scottish writer, brings dialect into play in the opening lines of his wonderfully dark novel, *How Late It Was, How Late.*

Ye wake in a corner and stay there hoping yer body will disappear, the thoughts smothering ye; these thoughts; but ye want to remember and face up to things, just something keeps ye from doing it, why can ye no do it; the words filling yer head; then the other words; there's something wrong; there's something far far wrong; ye're no a good man, ye're just no a good man. Edging back into awareness, of where ye are; here slumped in this corner, with these thoughts filling ye. And oh

christ his back was sore; stiff, and the head pounding. He shiv-
ered and hunched up his shoulders, shut his eyes, rubbed into
the corners with his fingertips; seeing all kinds of spots and
lights. Where in the name of fuck . . .

The dialect is inescapable, difficult and brilliant. Notice that it is not
pressed into dialogue in pieces, but instead it is the voice of the narrative consciousness. Dialect is the sound of the entire book. This is what
I meant earlier by narrative voice. The good reader has more patience
with it and accepts that the endeavor of picking up a novel like this is
to *feel* the language of it as part of the experience of reading it.

Why does this work, where that first "pie" dialect exchange does
not work? The sound of the voice is consistent and musical. The particular spellings are not thrown across the page ("spots and lights" could
have been spelled any number of ways to give in to this accent).
Throughout this novel, the voice of the dialect is an internal compo-
nent of the protagonist, Sammy, a Glasgow street person, who has
been brutalized by the state. This voice intertwines with a more direct
consciousness that works externally and more straightforwardly. Examine the following dialogue, which occurs in the first chapter of the
book after Sammy takes a beating by some soldiers and wakes up in
jail, blind. The book then becomes a story of voices, overwhelming at
times, but always clearly governed by a dual consciousness: the voice
of Sammy and the narrative voice.

His back, it was sore. The spine especially; down there at the
bottom, roundabout the lower ribs. He had to stand up. He
stood up. He stepped a pace to the left, then worked his hands
in where it was hurting, massaging with the tips of his fingers.
His right foot kicked against something metal.
Sit down. Samuels: sit down.
I need to stretch my legs.
Just sit on yer arse.
Can I no even get standing up?
Thirty seconds.
Thanks.
That's twenty of them.

Kelman does not overwhelm the reader with idiom and accent. No
intentional misspellings ("arse" actually appears in the British dic-

tionary by the way). Diction and syntax are manipulated to create these patterns. Here the dialect rises out of words, that is, sound and meaning, rather than mere sound. It works for that very reason. Kelman trusts the language. It is, after all, the language as he knows it. When writing dialect, that is your charge: *Trust the language as you know it.*

Environment means something. People who aren't heard, for instance, tend to speak louder, or to shut up entirely. But you should write to discover or uncover the environment and the tensions within it. Don't assume that the lower-middle-class family in which both parents work and are frazzled by debt is the spot where a child's voice might go unheard. Write to create a convincing circumstance and you might find that children go unheard in Martha's Vineyard just as they do in Tupelo. The idea is this: *Don't get sociological when shaping a character's voice.* Don't make presumptions as a writer about the way these environments work. There is nothing more icily calculated than a character whose words are used by the writer to take a poke at a social problem. Characters should speak, but only when they must, rather than when the writer needs them too. *Write dialogue to discover character rather than to reflect a set of givens.* In fact, push yourself to work against the givens and your dialogue will crank you into discovering entire stories as well as fully voiced characters.

I'm warning you about a pitfall here. These problems often come up when writers assume that accent, diction and use of slang define a character in some holistic fashion. They assume that writing dialect can bring them closer to the characters who speak in dialect. These writers often stumble forward, sacrificing character for a particular voice. The character's voice, and the presumptions behind it—quite often about race and class—becomes a mask, a scrim, between the character and the writer and, in the long run, the readers and the story in front of them.

There is no quicker way to fail, no quicker way to sell yourself short than to write unconvincing dialect. Your best intentions become mawkish charades. Readers are challenged not to live in your story, to get at the heart of what you have to say, but to "check" the loose strands of accent and spelling. It's one thing if you've spoken patois since childhood or if you grew up speaking the clunky street talk of

Brooklyn, but it's quite another when you assume to have mastery over the music and meaning of a dialect simply because you've heard it here and there. Here's a good watchword for dialect: *Do not use the language unless you live the language.*

CURSING

Kelman's book, like many others I read, is about full up with the word "fuck." You may think this word should never appear in print. That is your right. If so, I suggest you never print it. But whether you like this word or hate it, whether it's ugly or beautiful to you, it's a word that tends to leak its way into a lot of dialogue these days. Frankly, its frequency in our culture probably has a lot to do with the ocean of language we swim around in every day. Its history seems ancient to me. It was once used to shock, to shake up the status quo, to make people listen. Now, its life cycle in the lexicon is almost complete, as it represents little more than a lazy adjective, a dim frequency of anger. For some it remains a potent verb, an accented adjective, particularly when crossing lines of culture. Whether you banish the word from your stories or not, I think there's a way to think about cursing in general that can speak to dialogue writing in particular.

"Swearing," as we called it in my family, appealed to me as a boy in the distant way that adulthood seems glamorous to a child. It marked time. Soon I would be twelve, or fifteen, or eighteen and be able to use whatever sort of language I wanted. I listened with glee to the way adults put curses together. I looked forward to driving a car too and to getting my own place to live, but the ability to curse, and, more importantly, to curse well, seemed the blood rite of adulthood.

I spent blocks of time at the dinner table trying to figure out ways to insinuate the word "ass" into the evening conversation. It struck me as a dirty word but not so filthy as to send my mother for the wooden spoon. It was a testable word choice, a prime piece of new-found, eight-year-old diction, oily and ready for the speaking. I decided to use it casually in the course of telling a story at dinner. I waited until I had the corn on the cob completely buttered before I began.

"We were outside at lunch today," I said, taking a casual bite, "and Charlie Viles got stung by a hornet." I do not recall much reaction to my stories. They were generally true, though I often told them as a means of testing my parents' limits. My father, I think, favored a shrug, while my mother generally cued me along with another question, leading me, she hoped, to some reasonable point or revelation. Still they favored conversation, valued it as a linchpin of intelligent adulthood. After I told the part about the hornet, I distinctly remember a disinterested pause, which I knew I could fill right up for everyone's benefit. So I added, "Right on the *ass*."

My younger brother, who had been there for the stinging too, chimed in, "Right on the *butt*!"

"Bottom," my mother said. My father clinked his fork against his plate, stared at me.

"Ass," my youngest brother said. "Ass, ass, ass, ass." He sensed the power of the word too. I laughed. He was a good kid.

I waited for my father's response without looking at him. Only two weeks before, he had asserted the adult's privilege to words like this when my report card came back with three tardies. It was fresh in my mind. He had stared at the card, turned to my mother and said, "This really fries my ass! What the hell is tardy anyways? Why do they even keep track of tedious shit like that?" I was at the kitchen table then too, in the same chair where I would later float the word ass like a friendly weather balloon over the pork chops. My jaw dropped. Fried ass! What the hell! Tedious shit! Three straight sentences. Wham, bam, thank you ma'am! To my disappointment, my father downplayed his own transgression by focusing—unfairly I thought—on the fact that I couldn't get myself to school on time. But I remembered it well.

Now, after my own use of the word "ass," I hoped he would remember that he too was capable of multiple curses, without interruption, right here in our own kitchen. When I turned to look at him, he pointed a fork at me. "Don't say ass. You're not allowed that sort of language yet."

There. He had said it. *Yet.* Language like that had to be earned, by age, or experience, or brute task. Use of such language in conversation was a privilege. You had to earn it. I believe such is the case with good fiction. Never be lazy with the language. I know that is the case with good dialogue.

I'm not arguing that characters should be allowed to swear at every turn. Nor should they be encouraged to. The truth is, adults can't swear all the time. If they do, they tend to be looked on as pretty tedious shit. But they can, and do, swear. That's what my father was trying to tell me all those years ago. If they do it well, they choose their moments, pick their phrases and employ their wit. They grow into a use of language that suits them. That's how it should be with characters too.

The strong curse is

Pointed and precise. When you are dropping the word in out of habit, you've hit the point of too much. Hear it, precisely.

Quickly and forcefully crafted. Vary your use of words such as "fuck." Later in the book, I go on and on about adverbs and repetition. Same applies here. Shape and vary the language you use.

Revealing, both intentionally and unintentionally. Language (that is, diction) changes when emotions are charged. But that might be the moment where the swearing drops away. Work for the surprise.

These are the ways I'm encouraging you to create your dialogue. Good dialogue, whether windy or compressed, snappy or rambling, generally follows these principles. Like the good curse, strong dialogue lends shape to characters, even as the characters shape the words themselves.

ALL, BUT NOT EVERYTHING

If I'm going to give you any principle to lean on at all, it should be this one: *All, but not everything.* What I mean here is that we should be able to hear *all* that a character is through his words, but we don't have to hear *everything* he says. You are not a recorder. You are not trying to capture every word spoken. I hope I proved to you in the first chapter that capturing every word spoken does not make a story in itself. The story resides in smaller units, in the words themselves, in the moments of silence, in the pace and pause of exchange. All, but not everything.

Assume you have a character who is fond of exclamations such as "Golly gee" and "Gosh darn." Perhaps you are basing this character on a car dealer you know particularly well, and following my earlier advice, you have documented that this car dealer fellow uses the two words as often as forty times in a morning. That's all well and good, but you can't assume there's room for forty "Golly gees" in your story. Nor, more importantly, is there a need. These sorts of personal exclamations and catchphrases go a long way in a story. Remember rhythm. A well-timed "Gosh darn" goes a long way toward establishing who that character is. Unnecessarily sunny. Absurdly happy. Overly demonstrative. Genuinely nice. It could be any of these things, or all of them. Use catchphrases like this, time them well, but don't assume you are building a strong character because you lace your dialogue with personal exclamations. The same applies to idiomatic expressions. They tend to sound like blather when used too loosely.

Dialogue is one part of character. It should be consistent, well chosen and purposefully paced. Add too many catchphrases and the well-rounded character starts to flatten out like a crepe at high altitude. The principle of All, but not everything asks for inclusion of all that makes a character shine as himself, but at the same time demands a measure of this sort of thoughtful exclusion.

The same principle applies to cursing. The words "fuck" and "fucking" have got to be the most overused exclamations in the contemporary idiom. I hear them seventy times a day. On the golf course. On the basketball court. In the parking lot of the discount store. On the corner near the Centurion club, just as some guy is about to throw a bottle of malt liquor at the wheel of my car. When someone gets burned at the stove. When I nick myself shaving. On *The Dennis Miller Show*. When the Cubs lose. When the deficit rises. It seems to me that the only time I don't hear the word thrown around like a Handi Wipe at a convention of two-year-olds is when I'm at work, when I'm talking to my children or when I'm watching network television. I hope the first two will never change, but you never know what will happen with network television.

EXERCISES

1. I said diction rules. Let's prove it. Pick ten friends, preferably ten people from different parts of the country or the world. Ask them the same question, something easily answerable, but nothing that requires only a yes or no. Try for something open-ended enough that they will want to answer without asking more questions: Why should I have to know the nine planets? Aren't you sick of Michael Jordan? What would you do with a dead cat? Something they'll want to answer before they give you grief. Record the answers, with a tape recorder if you'd like. Now write the answers, word for word. Skip nothing. Read them back to yourself. Try to hear your friends' voices in the words, without imitating them. Pass the answers around and see if

your friends can recognize each other. Chances are many of them will say, "Only Red would say that," rather than, "Only Red would say it like that." Take a highlighter and mark the series of words that make each answer unique. Use one of the answers to begin a story. Now write a page or two that crafts a character around that answer, rather than around the friend who said it. Let the voice grow through your sense of character.

2. Translate one of your existing dialogues into a dialect you feel you know pretty well. Do it three times. On the first go-round, exaggerate the sound and accent of the words as much as possible. On the second run-through, use wholly correct spelling, but make the diction and syntax reveal the dialect. Then, in the third run-through, combine elements of the sound of language (that first translation) with the logic of language (the second dialogue). Combine both examples by taking an equal number of elements from each. What parts work better? Where does diction capture the rhythm? Where do accent and idiom more readily succeed?

FOUR

COMPRESSION

Apianist has recently had a small stroke. Weeks later it's clear that his hands, once the useful implements of his art, will betray him for the rest of his life. Doctors confirm that he's unlikely to ever make a full recovery. Now when he sits down to play, he finds himself, despite the best efforts of his therapists, his strength coach and his all-too-patient wife, just a beat or two behind, almost imperceptibly, but uncontrollably, off. Like any stroke victim, he has struggled to relearn the routine acts of everyday life—walking, talking, opening jars—and on these matters he has more than recovered. He cares nothing for the subtleties of speech and even less about walking without a limp. It is his hands he wants back. Fully and absolutely.

He works to improve his technique. All other signs of the stroke disappear quickly, and his music appears, to outsiders anyway, to improve greatly. Yet to his ear, it is slightly off, less than he is capable of. It is scarred and ugly, a constant reminder, not of what he possesses—as it had been all his life—but of everything he has lost.

In the meantime his life falls into shambles. He sinks into depression. He loses jobs, a concert tour falls through. He and his wife survive for a while on their savings, then on his disability income, but finally are in desperate straits. He must give up. He has to go out into the world and get a real job. He finds nothing, nothing he could ever love anyway. One night while working to frame some rare sheet music, a hobby taken up on the advice of his physical therapist, he fumbles with his project and drops it on the kitchen floor. His wife comes in to help him clean up. She speaks.

Before she speaks, let me pause here and say that this is a synopsis of a story a student presented to one of my workshops. We discussed the story in class at some length and afterward. There is, to be sure, an edge of melodrama to it. The timing is off too, as the character's descent into desperation is entirely too fast, as is his recovery (some six weeks all told). The writer was aware that she might be treading on certain clichés here, but she was interested in the story of a man who was the only one who could perceive changes in himself, changes that disturbed him so that they transformed him, from a gracious charming talent to a grumbling, groping has-been. She began the story nicely, with a focused image of his hands separating eggs for a cake batter. The narration slipped into a brief description of his music, of the act of playing as it felt and sounded to the protagonist, whose name was Jack. There was an awkward scene of him slamming the piano lid shut after a botched sonata (which the writer agreed was too much the clichéd act of a frustrated pianist and agreed to cut). From there the story moved unevenly across exposition and narrative with a limited amount of dialogue between Jack and his wife (with some fine moments in between) until the moment with the broken frame, which clearly was, to the writer's mind, the turning point of the story, if not something more.

In some ways this was a typical early draft of a story by a talented young writer. It was not a great story, but it was not a lousy one either. It had, as most early drafts do, its major weak spots, but it possessed strengths too. You may be holding your nose at the plot line, but it's probably more a matter of my poor synopsis than the flaws of the story itself. More importantly, as a teacher, I'm not going to kick somebody off her idea. That's not my job. You may think you've heard the same story told a thousand times—in movies, on television ("*M*A*S*H!*" you scream) or in your own life ("My cousin was a flutist until she broke her teeth in the spokes of my bike!"). Stories are constantly recycled. Journeys. Returns. Triumphs. Defeats. Change. Stasis. Writers shift the level of tension, the terms of the conflict and a new story is created from the bones of the old. Big news. But that's not the point. Readers of fiction (not to mention teachers of writing) have to accept that fact. Readers rely on it. These patterns keep us telling stories. So you live with it. The trick is to make each story unique with the echoes of your own voice, to show the details of the world in a way that convinces us we are seeing the core of it in front of us, perhaps for the first time.

Frankly, I liked the story of the pianist well enough just for the first scene, and I hung with it all the way, despite its flaws, until Jack sat down at the kitchen table. That's when the dialogue proper started up. Here's what followed, taken, with that wonderful student's permission, straight from her story.

"Jack," she whispered, "I just can't do this for much longer. I can't do it alone. Jack, I need you back."

"I know. God, Joan, don't you think I want to help? Don't you think I'm dying to have a purpose? I have lost everything that made me, me. Don't you see that. It's like starting over again."

"Why can't you just work like everyone else until we figure out what to do? I mean, can't you do that for me? Don't you love me enough for that? Don't you think I deserve that?"

"Of course you do. But you have to understand, delivering boxes of cookies to grandchildren and office supplies to businesses is not me. That's not what I do. And I don't have any solutions now. I'll think of something—I will."

"Jack, you are not a concert pianist. And you never will be. As terrible as that sounds, you have to learn that getting over it is the best thing you can do for yourself."

"I know, but just give me some time to figure out what I *can* do. Just give me a couple of weeks—maybe my hands will get better—"

"Jack, we don't have that much time to be wasting while you figure out what to do." Her voice faltered as she picked her hands from the floor and covered her face in them.

"What do you mean we don't have any time? We still have some savings from my last tour. We're not doing so badly, right?"

A piece of glass stuck in her forehead sent a drop of blood over her wrinkled hands. She uncovered her face. "Jack," she whispered, "I'm pregnant."

"What?" he stammered.

"Jack, we're pregnant and we need money for the baby. You need to go back to work tomorrow. I'm sorry but there isn't any other way."

"My God, how long have you known?"

"Since you had the stroke. I was going to tell you right after you got better. But then the arthritis came and I didn't think you could handle it. I wanted you to be happy. I wanted us to be happy. And six weeks ago I didn't think you could be happy."

"When were you going to tell me?"

"I just wanted you back on your feet again. And the doctors told me anything upsetting, any kind of responsibility, could trigger the depression. God, Jack, I didn't know what to do. I didn't know how you would react."

"Well, now I know it's over."

"What's over?"

"My dream. My dream to get it all back. My dream to concentrate on me for the first time in my life so I can achieve the only thing I ever really wanted."

"Well, it's good to know that's the only thing you ever really wanted."

She went to bed. And so did he.

Call this dialogue what you will. Stilted. Flabby. Wooden. Artificial. It's bad. My student called it that. She knew it didn't work. Heart and soul, she knew. Her story had been cranking right along too. Before this exchange, the characters were beginning to come into focus. Jack appeared to be puzzling it all out, deciding where he fit in, if he could change and how. His wife was tense about the massive disruption in their lives, but there was no reason to think she was hiding anything from Jack. The pacing of the scenes was fair. And, notably, the longest dialogue exchange up to that point was four or five lines. Then she started this dialogue and it flew out of her control. I told her I thought the dialogue was crappy, that the story fell apart at that point. She knew it didn't work even as she wrote it. But she still stuck it in there, hoping it could save the day for her story. To my mind, and I think to hers, it did quite the opposite. It sunk the story like a stone.

MAKING DIALOGUE DO TOO MUCH

What happened? For one thing, the writer tried to do everything with the dialogue. Look at this exchange closely. You'll find many of the structural elements of an entire story.

Exposition/setup: Things such as, "You are not a concert pianist." The mention of the stroke, the arthritis, the doctor's warnings, the dwindling money, the savings, the tour, the other jobs, the big news. The whole story is restated by the characters in this passage.

Conflict: Her "I need you" vs. his "I need more time." These are said, then said again and again.

Building tension: "I just can't do this for much longer." The tension in the dialogue comes from the frenetic pace as much as from the conflict between them.

Metaphor: The bit of glass in the forehead, the blood running over her hands. These are, notably, the only uses of scene within the dialogue. No where else do we see a detail from the kitchen. These moments are so dramatic, so melodramatic really, that they demand to be read metaphorically. The tiny cut is representative of the stroke; the blood on the hands represents his useless hands. This could work in a scene that was drawn together around other convincing details. Now they seem like bland, easily read metaphors taking the place of strong scenic detail. Too bad. They were pretty good images.

Climax/secondary tension: "I'm pregnant." Out of nowhere, the early concerns and tension are shot to pieces.

Realization/epiphany: "Well, now I know it's over." Not much of one, but a realization nonetheless.

Resolution: She went to bed. And so did he. And thank God they did too.

Their conversation as a believable piece of dialogue was over after a few lines. In fact, I might suggest it was done when his wife spoke those first lines, "I just can't do this for much longer. I can't do it alone. Jack, I need you back."

When Dialogue Fails

I would call this dialogue bloated. It's a lot of raw information to get into a scene, let alone into a series of convincing dialogue exchanges. You might be able to get that much story into a page and a half of text, and you might be able to come up with a circumstance in which you would want to, but, as I say elsewhere in this book, sometimes it's best just to shut up.

Clearly my student goes too far. There is excess throughout. The language has no rhythm to speak of. There is no physical dynamic at all, no tangible sense of scene working in any way to heighten, or even focus, the tensions in play. The dialogue breaks just about every rule I suggest here and in class.

What went wrong? The writer was trying to hinge her story on this conversation, to use it as a fulcrum for the tensions she'd balanced up to this point in the story. Would Jack fall apart? Or could he rise above this? The themes of the story were framed here in his words; look and you'll see his sense of self-worth, his identity, his reference point on the future. He may sound like an overindulged sot here, but he's got flashes of humanity in the things he says. He just goes on too long, as does she. And the more they speak, the more trouble they get themselves into. The student admitted that the pregnancy had at first been an attempt to knock some energy into the dialogue. I told her then it was the first thing that should go.

A Strategy for Bloated Dialogue

What can you do with dialogue like this? First, I might suggest that you try writing it. Yes. Try it. Elsewhere in this book I discuss stories that are nothing more than an extended dialogue. If you try to write an entire story in dialogue, you'll find you have a lot of obligations. Even if you decide to ignore scenic details—ambulances wailing, coffee rings on the table, the speckle of birds against the distant sky— you'll have to make the tension turn here and there. You have to do it in the spoken word. It's incredibly hard. But as you've discovered in your own writing, or maybe here in this book, there are ways to do it. It can be a burden, especially when the whole story is written with this conceit in mind.

So when you feel the whole story leaking away into a bit of expository dialogue, my first suggestion is don't stop yourself. Write every bit of it. Crank it out. Squeeze every sentence out of the mouths of the characters. Why give in, especially to what I'm suggesting is a bad habit? Well, don't let it become a habit. Just do it when you know things are falling apart. Sometimes this can be a helpful way of getting at the issues of the story. Perhaps you'll even find some conflicts you didn't recognize before.

But once you've felt what it's like to expand a story to its full bloat within a given dialogue, you'll see how dizzying expository dialogue can be. Just as with the "Brady-ized Dialogue" in chapter six, you can begin to feel you are writing for children, cueing the reader to each bump on the Oregon Trail of your logic. So finish it. Write every bit of it. Extend it to the point of absurdity. Then take these pages of dialogue to the side, pick up your red pen and get to work. Cut. Compress. Cut some more.

COMPRESSION

To defeat bloated dialogue, you have to learn to compress your language. Strip it to the barest bones. Cut everything. Use no gestures. No scene. (Not for now, anyway.) I told my student to rewrite the whole scene in five- or even three-word exchanges accompanied by only minimal scenic detail. I insisted that no character be allowed to speak more than five words at a time. Perhaps you think that can't be done. My student certainly thought that.

> "Five words?" she said, dumbfounded.
> "Five words," I repeated.
> "Come on."
> "I mean it," I said.
> "That's hard."
> "Compress."
> "There's a limit."
> "Sure there is."
> "Five words."
> "Five."
> "That's not natural."
> "Listen to yourself."

Get it? I'm using my old hat advice from chapter one here. Dig out the exercises in listening. Does anyone ever set her life up so completely as Jack and his wife do in their dialogue? Hell no. Remember your shorthand here. Words have meaning. Grant them that. Use them wisely. You give them more power when you *use words sparingly and in tension with other words*.

First, *figure out what each character wants*. There are few moments in life like the one between Jack and his wife, when needs and desires are being laid bare. Jack wants his life to be the way it was before. His wife wants their life to become what it might be. In a rhetorical sense, they are trying to persuade each other. Even if their emotions are not fully on the surface in this scene (and this is an issue the writer can decide later), there should be a sense of urgency in the things they say. Adhering to the three-words rule, at least for this draft, should help add that.

Second, *avoid exposition*. Remember that most relationships are held together with tacit threads, things unspoken. Jack and his wife are married, so it's easy to see that they would know their history, that they would know the other's argument even as it's being made. But this advice holds true for most relationships and, notably, for most dialogue.

Consider this scene. A waiter comes to the table. A customer peruses the menu. Almost every element of the relationship is tacitly evident in the first words spoken: "What can I get you this evening?" They both know what's up. They understand and accept what's about to transpire. They both want things (the waiter, a clear order and generous tip; the customer, good service and hot food), but they don't state the entire circumstance either.

> "Hello," said the waiter. "Have you had enough time to look at the menu, that piece of heavy-stock paper embossed with the full range of choices we offer in the three major categories— appetizer, entree and desserts—as well as a drink menu and sundries on the back there? I decided to see if you were ready to order now because I had a lull and I'm hoping to get this order started before I start on that guy's Caesar salad, which is an awful hassle since we use real anchovies and I have to peel open a new tin every time I make one. What a nightmare! At the very least, you might be ready to order a drink now from our full-service bar, which is right over there, just past that brass rail, next to the entrance."

If the world were full of waiters like this, we'd all be ready to eat at home a lot more. But in some ways he's telling it like it is. The truth is, it's actually kind of nice that a person doesn't state everything he wants, everything he knows and everything both of you accept every time he speaks to you. Dialogue often becomes bloated with exposition, by the need to remind the reader of the basic tensions at work, to explain the circumstance beyond what is realistic and necessary. There's a false triangle many writers get trapped in. In this paradigm, the writer sees the characters talking for the benefit of the reader, as if the characters were speaking essentially to the reader.

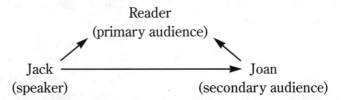

In the false triangle, the reader is the primary audience, the one for whom the words are being spoken. Thus, dialogue is shaped to the needs of the reader, rather than to those of the other character. Dialogue directed in this fashion sounds phony because it is phony. These aren't people talking. These are people "demonstrating" conflict or "actualizing" tension. The dialogue sounds wooden because its conceit is self-congratulatory. The writer who embraces this way of doing things suggests that the world he depicts is a cheap gauze, a mere filter for his ideas. If you are trying to write convincing, compelling stories, the relationship between the characters ought to be your primary concern.

What is the real model? Well, I hate models. They remain best written upon blackboards, where they can be erased, turned into dust by whoever happens along next. Still, there is probably a way to understand the relationship better by looking at a revised version of the false triangle. In this version, the energy of meaning runs from the reader, as secondary audience, toward both the character and the words themselves.

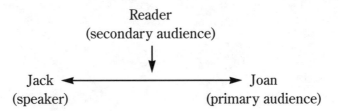

In this version, the meaning moves in more than one direction, and the reader is given some responsibility in the process. Here the reader looks at the conversations themselves for meaning, as well as the characters. The key is not to think of models as ways to succeed in crafting your dialogue. Remember, characters speak to each other, not to the reader.

Let's return to compression. Remember *tension means rhythm, and rhythm means interruption.* When you are compressing, you can pull a dialogue together by using the rhythm of the exchange to your advantage. Allowing characters to interrupt one another, to complete sentences, to repeat each other, is a way of reflecting the two items discussed earlier: what they want and what they know. When you are consciously boiling things down, the way you are in the act of compression, you have to rely on rhythm, interruption and flow within a dialogue. I'm telling you to go to five-word exchanges. You will get stuck. When you're stuck on which five words to use, have one character change the subject briefly or abortively. Or let one character cut the other one off in midstream. Or think of one as an echo for the other in a given moment. The exchanges in compressed dialogue ought to be like drums speaking to one another.

RHYTHM

Think in terms of beats. Read the following exercise, but while doing it, pound your left hand on the desk in beat with one character's lines, pound your right hand in beat with the other's. Use the number of words to represent the number of beats.

Left: You're drunk.
Right: I'll drive.
Left: Not with me.
Right: I'm hungry.
Left: Don't touch me.
Right: I'll drive.
Left: You'll drive.
Right: Yes.
Left: What do you want?
Right: Pancakes.
Left: Stop it.
Right: What?
Left: You smell.
Right: I've been drinking.
Left: I said—
Right: Just get in.
Left: You smell. Leave me be.

This has snap. Inferences can be drawn from it. It's not the whole story, absolutely not. But a lot of the story is in here, in this moment. Notice the techniques employed in this short space: repetition, interruption, changing the subject and echoing. There's very little exposition ("I've been drinking" qualifies, I suppose). There's also a clear sense of what each person wants, and not just in the moment, but perhaps beyond. The physical dynamic is clear enough. They are standing next to a car ("Just get in."). He might be coaxing (her "Don't touch me" line indicates his reaching for her to calm her). Her anger and his drunkenness are indicated in the way she echoes him ("You'll drive.") and the way he cuts her off.

Not every conversation is this punchy or brief. You have to recognize that. But remember what you are teaching yourself by clipping down to this kind of pow-pow exchange. Compression. You are mastering tight, highly expressive exchange. This is not banter either. These are people talking. By just barely saying anything, they are saying everything. Against your best instincts, you have to remind yourself that less is more, that you are meeting your obligations far more artfully by holding back than you would by lathering it on.

In Tobias Wolff's autobiography, *This Boy's Life*, are many examples of compressed dialogue. Look at the following dialogue without being introduced to the larger context of the book or the more particular one of this conversation. How much of it can you put together? The speaker is the narrator of the book, who likes to be called Jack.

> I was up on the school roof with Chuck. He was looking at me and nodding meditatively. "Wolff," he said. "Jack Wolff."
> "Yo."
> "Wolff, your teeth are too big."
> "I know they are. I know they are."
> "Wolf-man."
> "Yo, Chuckles."
> He held up his hands. They were bleeding. "Don't hit trees, Jack. Okay?"
> I said I wouldn't.
> "Don't hit trees."

What sorts of things can you infer about these two? How old are they? What are they doing? What sort of relationship do they have?

I'm about to give you the answers, so think before you read on. All of the answers can be taken from this dialogue alone.

Well, they're kids, teenagers. Notice how Chuck ribs the narrator, the use of nicknames. They're on a roof, blowing each other grief. Chuck has been hitting trees. The sort of thing a boy does when he's fourteen or fifteen and has been drinking, which is what the two of them have been doing.

Now read the dialogue again, with the particulars of context better drawn out. Are things better focused? Maybe a bit, but essentially the dialogue is give-and-take, a back-and-forth, mostly reflective of an attitude. In some ways, it is a clean representation of how lost the narrator was at this moment in his life, when he felt cut off from his mother, isolated and alone in a tiny logging town and headed in all the wrong directions. It is not the whole story. There is no attempt to summarize the event. There is no long look at Chuck, no direct statement of how drunk he is. The words the boys speak do the work. Yet there is very little substance to what they say (which is surely part of the point) except for "Don't hit trees." How does this dialogue run? Repetition, interruption, echoing and changing the subject are all evident.

Here's another example of compressed dialogue, this one from Bobbie Ann Mason's "Shiloh." In this story, a working-class woman named Norma Jean goes through a crisis of self-identity and feels her marriage has left her trapped. At the end of the story, she and her husband, Leroy, picnic on the battlegrounds at Shiloh. There, surrounded by the monuments and forests, far from their trailer, Norma Jean says, "I want to leave you." The dialogue that follows is both predictable and surprising, and it stands as a good example of successful compression.

> Without looking at Leroy, she says, "I want to leave you."
>
> Leroy takes a bottle of Coke out of the cooler and flips off the cap.
>
> He holds the bottle poised near his mouth but cannot remember to take a drink. Finally, he says, "No, you don't."
>
> "Yes, I do."
>
> "I won't let you."
>
> "You can't stop me."

"Don't do me that way."

Leroy knows Norma Jean will have her own way. "Didn't I promise to be home from now on?" he says.

"In some ways, a woman prefers a man who wanders," says Norma Jean. "That sounds crazy, I know."

"You're not crazy."

Leroy remembers to drink from his Coke. Then he says, "Yes, you are crazy. You and me could start all over again. Right back at the beginning."

"We have started all over again," says Norma Jean, "and this is how it turned out."

"What did I do wrong?"

"Nothing."

"Is this one of those women's lib things?" Leroy asks.

"Don't be funny."

The cemetery, a green slope dotted with white markers, looks like a subdivision site. Leroy is trying to comprehend that his marriage is breaking up, but for some reason he is wondering about white slabs in a graveyard.

"Everything was fine till Mama caught me smoking," says Norma Jean, standing up. "That set something off."

What you might notice here is how much less evasion is evident in this one. The pattern of interrupting exists, but the two characters stay on the subject, dealing with it in an amazingly small number of exchanges. This is a literal compression; words are squeezed out of the lines, until the expression is at its barest and clearest. By moving things toward the most minimal exchange possible, you begin to discover the marvelous potential of economy in language. Get this down and then you can release. Compress and release. Compress and release. Sounds like a birthing class. But we'll get to that later.

A REWORKED DIALOGUE

What did my student, the one with her pianist story, come up with on her five-word exchange exercise? She made some easy plot changes, getting rid of the arthritis, extending his recovery period to over a year, losing the pregnancy altogether. Still the conversation had weight. One week later she came back to me with this. Remember, the wife has walked in just after he has fumbled with the frame.

His wife walked in, threw her keys on the table and regarded the mess. "What is this?"

"Nothing," he said.

"It looks like something," she said.

"You have no idea."

"I live here, Jack."

"You couldn't have any idea."

"What's that supposed to mean?"

"How could you?"

"I am living in the miserable world you created."

"Great, thanks for your support."

"I don't know what to do anymore."

"Fall in love with me again."

"I am in love with you."

I stopped reading there. This new section starts out pretty tight. It's far more tense, and the distance between them is more tangible. There is a gap between them; they aren't explaining to each other, at least not at first, but are merely talking to each other. But they begin explaining to each other as soon as she asks him directly, "What's that supposed to mean?" That is just a clever way of explaining to the readers, of answering their questions. Remember that in life, conversations do not go on for the sake of an audience.

What the writer doesn't see is that there's no need to explain yet. The tension isn't high enough. The wife has only been home for about two minutes. It's too soon to be laying it all out there. More than anything, it's indicative of the fact that the writer has lost her balance and is trying to find it by allowing the dialogue to explain her way out of things. Besides she'd broken my five-word rule too many times to say that she'd really worked at compressing. I sent her off, and she came back a day later. This time it looked like this. Again, the wife is regarding the broken glass when she begins.

Her: What's this?

Him: Nothing.

Her: Looks like something.

Him: You have no idea.

Her: None.

Him: You should know.

Her: I should.
Him: Yes, you should.
Her: I don't.
  (He nodded.)
Her: But I live here.
Him: Yes.
Her: Me. Us. I live here.
Him: What's that supposed to mean?
Her: I want to.

The question appeared again! But this time it worked, because she wasn't answering a question that could sum up the story. She was answering a question for her husband and she was saying, *indirectly*, that she loved him and that she wanted to help. To my mind, the dialogue has come miles by this point. The exchanges, despite some obvious flaws, show real improvement. The tensions are better focused in the writer's mind. Again, I stopped at this point, reading no further. But there were pages of this stuff. My student complained that it had gotten too long. I assured her this was no problem unless she was unwilling to cut. "Cut more?" she said.

Yes. Compression has many stages. I urged her to go through and look for longer passages. Again, she fell into a pattern of ignoring my five-word rule. Things like this appeared later.

"I'm just so tired of walking around here like it's a mortuary. There is life out there, Jack. A life that's waiting for you. A life that just might not be so bad. But you just can't bring yourself to look for it."

Compressed, that might look like this.

"There is a life out there for you."

Here's another exchange.

Him: A part of me has died. Can't you understand that?
Her: Of course. I mean I know how much your music meant to you. It's just been so long since your stroke.

It can be compressed into this.

Him: Part of me died.
Her: Of course. I mean I know. It's just been so long.

I told her to pluck out the most well-compressed lines from the entire seven pages and see what happened when she slapped them together. She was doing this from over six pages of double-spaced dialogue. I told her to fit it all into fifteen to twenty exchanges. I told her to release the five-word rule when she needed to, but to use it just one more time as a watchword. This is what she came up with.

> Her: What's this?
> Him: Nothing.
> Her: Looks like something.
> Him: It's a job. I was doing a job.
> Her: You dropped . . .
> Him: It broke. I was working and it broke.
> Her: I know you were working.
> Him: You have no idea.
> Her: None.
> Him: You should know.
> Her: I should.
> Him: Yes, you should.
> Her: I don't.
> (He nodded.)
> Her: But I live here too.
> Him: What's that supposed to mean?
> Her: I want to. I want to know.
> Him: I've done this. I broke this. (He motioned to the glass.)
> Her: I just wish you wouldn't sit here like somebody died.
> Him: Part of me did die.
> Her: Of course. (She knelt down next to him, brushed the broken glass from his sleeve.) I mean I know. It's just been so long.
> Him: No one could know. No one could possibly know.
> Her: I know. We know.
> Him: There is a life. I can see it.
> Her: There is.
> Him: It's just hard.

Now is this new dialogue all that much better? Maybe. I certainly think so. It needs some scene to be sure. That will help with the pace. It's still melodramatic as all get-out. Frankly, I'd like her to leave him hanging. My bent as a writer is to avoid easy resolutions, since I find so few of them in my own life. But that's a question of aesthetic, of the writer's ideas, and this is not my story.

But go all the way back to that first version. In this new draft, far less is revealed, far less direction is lent to the dialogue. Despite its relative speed, it feels more natural, more like people talking to each other. Beyond that it doesn't pin the writer into any new corners. This dialogue is not perfect, but if the writer keeps pushing the story outward now, toward the scene, it will be complete in the sense that this is all the characters have to say to each other in order for the reader to come closer to them and their story.

WATCHWORDS FOR COMPRESSION
Write this on an index card.

> Figure it out.
> Cut it out.
> Read it out.
> Turn it out.

Use that card when you're working to compress a bloated dialogue. Do you know what it means?

Figure it out: Know what the characters want and need. You don't have to tell it. In fact, you shouldn't. But you do have to figure them out. These desires, these needs are the tacit motivation for speaking. They are why we ask. They are why we tell.

Cut it out: Write whatever kind of dialogue you want. Be as explicit as you need yourself to be. But then cut it to the barest bones. Have faith in the cuts you make. Be sure the core of the dialogue is clear expression. Cut everything you can, even as you are typing it. Compress.

Read it out: Read the dialogue aloud. You don't have to be an actor. But you should be able to hear the voices at work. You ought to be able to tap out the dialogue in your own voice, even if the character is someone from an entirely different world. This is part of understanding character and prose. Reading aloud is a must. If you haven't begun reading your work aloud yet, get yourself to a fiction reading.

You'll probably find that the fiction writer takes most care when reading his dialogue. That's the sort of care you should be giving your work as well.

Turn it out: By this I mean two things. Once you've cut to the barest bones, once you're onto the real rhythms, release the dialogue a little. Allow a speaker to clarify, or maybe backtrack a little. To help you here, think of the techniques I gave you: repetition, interruption, changing the subject and echoing. These things can help to extend the focal points of a dialogue.

When I say turn it out, I also mean turn the dialogue out into the physical world. Use the details of the world to refract the dialogue. Cars honking. Animals braying. Plates breaking. Tears falling. Snorts. Bells. Whistles. Chest thumping. Imperceptible twitches. Stomachaches. Corn flakes underfoot. The smell of spray paint in the air. Details are what make stories their own particular brand of pleasure, and the same is true of dialogue. Once you've trimmed to the essential, you've made much room for the physical world or gesture and circumstance. Take some pleasure in turning the dialogue outward.

EXERCISES

1. *Decompress.* Take a brief dialogue from one of your stories. It could start out as a short (no more than four or five exchanges), highly contextualized dialogue—something a new reader would be able to make neither heads nor tails of, the kind you might call "throwaway dialogue," at least now. Pluck it from the story as a whole, and rewrite it as the whole story. Decompress the entire story into this conversation. Remember your obligations: You have to create clear exposition, you have to draw the story toward certain themes and you have to use the dialogue to advance the plot. See what you can do in a relatively short space, say two pages, but go on if you must.

2. *Compress.* Below you will find an example of bloated dialogue. Compress the dialogue using the techniques discussed. *Determine what the characters want or need. Avoid exposition. Discover the tension,* remembering tension means rhythm. Run with these. Go where you need to. Add details that make it more compelling. Employ actions that are well chosen, surprising and realistic, that is, no sudden foghorns in the middle of a church in Tempe. (Suspend your disbelief on your

own time, bud.) Remember, compressed language strikes a certain pattern, but in search of the pattern, you must cut. Try rewriting this in five-word exchanges. How few can you cut it to without losing meaning?

"Oh, Jenny," he whispered. "I'm unhappy. I mean, it's not that you don't mean a lot to me. You do mean a lot to me, a whole lot. Back in Tucson that time was special. I mean it. I meant it then too." He shifted in his pew.

"I bet," Jenny said, loud enough so that people started leaning in to eavesdrop. "Rob, ever since you went and joined the army two years ago, just because of the Gulf War, I have been living in that little crappy house with my parents, waiting for you to come back and tell me that you loved me. You said you wanted to marry me when we were on the water slide at Kings Island. Do you remember that much? My friends all have good jobs now. They've taken the best jobs in this town. And now you're running off on this hair-brained scheme to sell T-shirts out of the back of your '78 van, the one your parents customized? You were in the army. Don't you have more pride than to sell T-shirts out of the back of a van?"

"Not just T-shirts. Embroidered T-shirts. And I'm not selling them out of the van. I'm just using the van to make deliveries. I took the refrigerator out to make more room. Besides, I do love you. That was no lie. I'm just a little lost now is all."

"When I think of that van I just think of all the good times, Rob."

"I know, me too. Like the time at the reservoir before the tournament? Remember that? When Jesse Hocken fell in that spillway."

"How could I forget?"

"I'm under a lot of pressure. The bank has an eye on me. My parents are watching. I just have to make a go of this. I'm just asking you to give me some time to get this embroidered T-shirt thing off the ground."

"Yes, Rob. I will. But I have to tell you that six months is a long time. You will be out on the road, living the high life. Don't expect me to sit by and play the loyal girlfriend. I'm too worried about my future now. I feel very uncertain and lost."

"I thought we were getting married."

"You probably did think we were going to get married. You could have had the church picked out for all I care. That's exactly what I think you're always talking to your mother about," Jenny said. A man next to them shushed her. "Oh you hush! I'm talking about my time in Tucson here and it's very painful. I'm just happy to be back here in Tempe."

3. *Engineer.* Write a bloated dialogue, along the lines of exercise one. Now work like a compression engineer. If you are in a class, you could exchange dialogues to do this. If you are working alone, locate a long, windy dialogue within a book you know. You can stand in a bookstore and thumb through books until you find one. It's amazing how many are out there. Writers can be impressively self-indulgent.

When you are acting as the compression engineer, or editor, the challenge is to compress without losing meaning, or without violating the spirit of the exchange. Don't add details. Just use the words in front of you. You may heighten voice or tinker with pace. These changes are a must. But press on the original dialogue until there are only five-word exchanges left. The original writer should reread his dialogue with the compression engineer, each taking a voice. The two of them together will more than likely find even more places to cut and compress.

ON SILENCE

Look at the Sunday comics. Everybody's got a bubble of her own, and words crowd it to the max. Every page, bubble after bubble. In the really talky strips—the serials such as "Rex Morgan, M.D." and "The Phantom"—many of the panels have more than one bubble in each. It's a bubble-rama. Everyone talking, filling his bubble. More than that, every panel and every bubble has a purpose: the setup, the buildup, the punch line and the reaction. Crystal clear. Some artists even manipulate these bubbles for each stage of the process. Considerate bastards.

The dialogue in Sunday comic strips is worth studying. It barrels forward because it must. In the serials, exposition is a part of every exchange; readers have to tune in the tensions quickly. Therefore, each exchange is likely to begin with a reminder ("You may have Kat tied up in the backseat of you car, but you've forgotten that I've had a set of spare keys since our run-in with Dr. Develin!") and end with an unresolved crisis ("Have you mentioned that to Red?"). This stuff could never work in fiction, except as camp, but then again, fiction writers don't have to ink all those bubbles either.

So what's to learn? Economy for one thing. There you can begin to see that space and time are an issue in dialogue. As in fiction, language is the premium. The comic strip writer can't flap on and on, nor can he allow his characters to do so. An intelligent, focused use of language wins out again and again. While each strip may rely on its own formula, it's important to realize this is a constraint for the writer as much as it is an assurance. These writers may not have to create realistic dialogue, but then again they are rarely given the space to try it. Those who succeed manage to mix voice, gesture and circumstance in so few words that the sheer economy ought to be praised by fiction writers, if not imitated.

But look at a page and all you see are bubbles. Read too much of that stuff and the temptation is to give in to the bubble mentality. In fiction, this refers to the understandable instinct to include dialogue in every "moment" of the story, as if each scene, half-scene, flashback demands the voice of each character. But, listen, this is a hard one: *Sometimes you have to shut up.*

QUIET DOWN

In this chapter, I'd like to talk about two ways of shutting up. *Quieting a character* is perhaps the easiest to grasp. Often it's a matter of trying not to answer questions with dialogue but with action. There are also ways to quiet one character within the literal dialogue to let another character take over: understanding that no response is sometimes the best response, shifting the focus at the moment we most expect to hear something, avoiding the temptation to be overly explicit, forcing the physical world into play at surprising moments. Another element of silence is *quieting the narrative*, a form of stripping your dialogue to the bare bones for the sake of focus or pace. It does not require a quiet setting, merely a setting that drops away for a time, allowing the dialogue to take over. The writer quiets the narrative presence. You shut yourself up in a manner of speaking so that only the dialogue exchange stands on the page, unadorned by external detail or tension.

In any case, it's a question of learning to value the instinct to say less, to trust the story and its various silences. In a book about writing dialogue, a book that concerns itself with filling the unseen bubbles of fiction with good words, this message on silence might be the most important of them all.

SILENCE AS RESPONSE

There are moments when silence comes naturally to a character or scene. In these cases, silence seems the natural answer, an extension of the exchange between two people. Let's look at Chekhov's masterpiece "The Lady With the Pet Dog" again. Gurov, the married Muscovite, and his new love, Anna Sergeyevna, walk on the pier. They have only recently met, and, drawn to each other from the start, they are on their way to a painful and wonderful sort of love. In the scene below, notice how persistent and natural Anna's silence seems.

> The festive crowd began to disperse; it was now too dark to see people's faces; there was no wind any more, but Gurov and Anna Sergeyevna still stood as though waiting to see someone else come off the steamer. Anna Sergeyevna was silent now, and sniffed her flowers without looking at Gurov.
>
> "The weather has improved this evening," he said. "Where shall we go now? Shall we drive somewhere?"
>
> She did not reply.
>
> Then he looked at her intently, and suddenly embraced her and kissed her on the lips, and the moist fragrance of her flowers enveloped him; and at once he looked round anxiously, wondering if anyone had seen them.
>
> "Let us go to your place," he said softly. And they walked off together rapidly.

Anna's silence is as sure a response to their impossible love as any words Chekhov might have chosen. Twice within this section, silence is the trigger for Gurov; twice it pulls him forward better than any spoken invitation. Here, silence beckons stronger than words.

There are moments when nothing can be said. Many things might stand behind this sort of silence. Pain. Conflict. Resolve. Here, the person stops speaking because silence is the only answer. Silence *is* the response. Notice that Chekhov isolates Anna's silence into a one-line paragraph. This is the most familiar example of silence—silence as statement. Although the occasion for it is uncommon, this kind of silence is the most easily rendered.

CHOOSING SILENCE OVER WORDS

But what about when people are talking? What about when a conversation is simply flying along? How do you know when to turn off the spigot of jabber? Other times, when you're sitting in front of your computer screen, pushing your way through a tough stretch, it can feel like you are dredging words from a character. What then? It is often tempting to wait until you simply hear the words loft themselves from the mouth of your hero. You know what I say. Often that's just the thing to do. Listen and wait.

Assume you're writing a scene in which two brothers are arguing in a bar. They reach a moment during which the younger brother will reveal his secret. Say he stole money from his brother at a low point and since then he's felt himself in a spiral. You lean back in your chair and decide to let the conversation make the choice. You wait to hear the words of the younger brother, to feel for the tension in what he says next. You expect it to come easily. The story has been building toward this for days now. But hours pass. Then it is time for your dinner and you're going dancing later! So you run the conversation in your head for several days until you hear any number of words and dozens of exchanges between them that never quite focus the moment between the brothers. Hold on. What if the brother didn't speak? What if he held the secret? What if he said nothing?

In another section of this book, I might tell you quite the opposite. Just put it on the page, I'd say. Be honest. Be direct. Trust the words. All of that is good advice. Sometimes that's just the thing, but not always. Maybe there's another way to continue this exchange. Work against your expectations of what should be said. Say less. Say nothing. Let the scene take the weight.

Here's a different example. Say two boys are walking through the woods. They have collected a handful of mushrooms, against the wishes of their mother. One boy has goaded the other into it for reasons he won't reveal. As they walk, they debate about what to do with the mushrooms now that they've collected them.

"You know they're poison," Kelly said. "You know it."

Jim pulled up on the barbed wire fence and motioned for Kelly to pass under. "Go on."

Kelly stepped under and held the wire for Jim. "I just want to drop them right here. What if the poison's right here, on our hands?"

"That ain't so. The poison's in the mushroom. You got to eat it."

"Yeah. But one bite. That's all. We should have a bag. We shouldn't be walking. This could be leaking right through my skin right now." He held a mushroom between his thumb and forefinger.

"That is stupid. Don't be that way."

"It can happen."

"Can not. Just 'cause you say it, doesn't mean it's a fact."

They stepped over a log and stopped. To their right a twig broke. Kelly dropped a mushroom. Jim wiped his nose on his sleeve. "I want to kill Pearson's dog," he said.

Kelly shook his head and picked up the mushroom. Then he stepped forward and Jim followed.

There. Just at the moment you would expect the debate between them to get hotter, the scene veers into silence. That's a good example of letting the scene, or the moment, take the weight. It was not the moment I intended when I began this scene, which I took from one of my notebooks. But my sense is the silence served me well, as Kelly gains some element of power by not speaking. I decided to let them keep moving, to allow the plot to trip forward, to work a bit more with the place, to let the characters stew. I discovered the moment by allowing silence to be the equal of words.

Surprise yourself with silence. This is not a means of surprising the reader necessarily; this is about you, the writer. It's about rendering a moment, about picturing it even as it happens. Strangely, this is just another form of trusting the words.

In the worst sort of dialogue, answers are provided for the reader more than for the character; there, resolution comes more for the shape of the story than for the shape of the characters. Go back to the two brothers in the bar. If the reader has known the brother's secret for fifteen pages, is there any drama in stating it now? Perhaps, if what the writer wants is the reaction of the other brother. Doesn't silence press harder against the tension the reader feels? Doesn't it offer the possibility of something tacit, something deep and unstated between the brothers, rising up to fill the moment? If the story is close to its end, shouldn't the resolution be more than flicking a switch with a line of dialogue? Certainly.

Remember, *your reader is a secondary audience to dialogue.* The primary audience for a line of dialogue is the character himself. As such he has a different set of knowledge, usually far more limited, than the reader does.

The character within the story ought not to speak from within the story so much as from within his life. A character doesn't know anything about resolution. He don't need your stinking resolution. If he's a real person, a real character, he's speaking so he can go on, or because he can't, not because the story is near an end.

When a character goes silent, holds back or turns away in a moment like that, much is revealed. That silence stands as an act in itself. That silence might heighten tension or provide resolution, signal a parting of ways or, by contrast, an agreement. Sometimes the answer lies in not speaking, in keeping quiet.

FILLING THE SILENCE

But consider moments of silence in your life, moments when two or more people are gathered and no one speaks. To be sure, there are not many of these in the average day. For most of us, there aren't enough. Waiting at the bus stop maybe. The silent prayer in church. The pause before tee-shot. The counter at the half-empty coffee shop. The subway ride in a strange city. While some of these moments may be quiet, none of them is silent (not even saying the prayer), and not a one of them is still. The world moves in moments like this, the physical dynamic between human beings swirls along.

The silence I'm referring to is not a vacuum. Things happen. You must find ways to fill the silence reliably and convincingly. The different types of gesture encompass an array of options. Recognizing the function of place, or scene, reveals another set of possibilities.

Gesture

But what fills the empty space when characters go quiet while the scene persists? It's a bit trite to say that conversation is more than words, but at its core, you're looking at a series of exchanges, both verbal and physical. When the words stop, the physical world does not dry up. Cigarettes are offered. Eyes shift. Hands run through hair. Fingers tap tabletops. People wave for waiters. Kisses are given. Each of these gestures can be as significant within a dialogue as any spoken words. Often more so.

We've already noted that physical gestures can and should play a role in dialogue, in what is being said and how. But they can also be used to fill the silence. Used well, they ought to define it. There are different gestures a writer can employ. Each is useful in nagging a difficult dialogue along. Some cut straight to the meaning of the conversation; others are particular to character; others, still, are incidental to the circumstance.

Dramatic gesture. A dramatic gesture is one in which the gesture itself is designed to have meaning that reinforces the human exchange. Sometimes these are simple clichés. A woman stubs her cigarette out in an ashtray after she finishes dumping her boyfriend. An executive swats a fly on his desk as he fires an employee. A boy's eyes grow shifty as he lies to his father about stealing cars. These are the sorts of gestures we see in bad television. They are visual cues, dramatic clichés and little more. Frankly, unless intended to exaggerate a moment to the brink of comedy or cliché, they are better left unused.

Using dramatic gestures successfully is a question of lifting the movement out of the realm of the stock, the familiar. Quite often it might border on cliché, but the successful dramatic gesture rises above that. It particularizes a human condition, just as a story describes one. It may be symbolic at its core, but to the reader, the strong dramatic gesture is specific to the story. In Raymond Carver's wonderful story "A Small, Good Thing," the parents of a boy who dies from the consequences of a hit-and-run accident are hounded by a baker who has been left with an unpaid account on the boy's birthday cake. The baker makes crank phone calls, which the mother receives while the boy is hospitalized and later after he dies. At first she can't make the connection and has no idea who is calling, but at last she figures it out. She and her husband confront the baker in his kitchen early one morning. He is horrified at his callous mistake. He begs their forgiveness, then asks them to sit and have some coffee. He then offers them bread, calling up communion, images of nurturing, healing human rituals. Offering the bread is a fine example of a dramatic gesture.

> "You probably need to eat something," the baker said. "I hope you'll eat some of my hot rolls. You have to eat and keep going.

Eating is a small, good thing in a time like this," he said.

He served them warm cinnamon rolls just out of the oven, the icing still runny. He put butter on the table and knives to spread the butter. Then the baker sat down at the table with them. He waited. He waited until they each took a roll from the platter and began to eat. "It's good to eat something," he said, watching them. "There's more. Eat up. Eat all you want. There's all the rolls in the world here."

It's not the level of drama that defines the dramatic gesture, it's the potency. This small moment harkens to the idea of providing and protecting. It's a sort of communion between the characters, a ritual of forgiveness. The gesture takes on a level of significance because it speaks to all parts of the story and to other larger stories of the world. There's no sense trying to calculate these moments in advance. A dramatic gesture succeeds when it grows from inside the story. You'll have to learn how to turn up the gas when the moment is right. The point is not to grope around for the right symbolic gesture but to teach yourself to trust gesture and recognize drama.

Particular gesture. Easier to craft and more useful perhaps is the particular gesture, which involves a movement or action unique to an individual. A woman who touches the top button of her blouse before she speaks. A man who holds both hands out in front of him, fingers pinched together, as he sings. These sorts of things are all around you. Your friends are a wellspring of these tics and triggers. You have to be a wickedly precise observer to train yourself to zero in on particular habits. I once played softball with a guy who slapped himself on the forehead with two fingers before he would recount a bad fielding play. My brother droops one shoulder when he lies. My wife sometimes pulls paper napkins into tiny squares when she is finished eating. Observing pays off in other ways too. I've played poker for years with a history professor who wraps his fingers around the edge of his cards when he's holding a good hand and keeps them flat on the back of the cards when his hand is shit. (Sorry, John.)

Obviously these gestures are directly connected to individuals, and as such are useful in any exchange between characters, even when they are not speaking. The movements your characters invent, favor or rely upon are as much a part of them as the words they choose. So don't merely *listen* and wait, *watch* the character too.

The beauty of particular gestures is that they are easy to find in the life around you. Try watching a conversation from a distance great enough that it keeps you from hearing what's being said, but not so far that you can't see these small exchanges taking place. Take note of every tiny movement. The shifting of weight from foot to foot. The brief glance into the distance. The arm clamping the briefcase to the chest. Even while talking directly to another person, you can pick up new details. It's odd to talk to someone you've known for years and notice for the first time that he chews his gum from side to side. Still it's something you've seen all along, a part of dozens of past conversations between the two of you, and you hadn't noticed. You might begin to feel that your eyes are trespassing, but watch closely for changes in expression. How the face moves! The longer you look, the more you will find.

A human being controls more than language when speaking. Conversation is a matter of balance and direction, muscle control and manners. Readers will remember the particular gesture, rising out of a real character, long after they forget the dramatic one, calculated for mere effect.

Incidental gesture. The incidental gesture is useful in turning the dynamic outward toward the setting or circumstance. The grave robber bats the gnats from his face as he scratches the dirt off the top of the coffin. The little boy plugs his ears as the ambulance whips past. The woman quietly returns a nod from across the restaurant. These sorts of things can be helpful with timing and rhythm. Quite often these gestures are a matter of setting and circumstance.

Let's go back to the brothers at the bar. What are the typical ambient noises in a bar? List them from most to least obvious. The jukebox. The cash register. The clicking of the balls on the pool table. A group of people laughing at a joke. A bell behind the bar, rung loudly on a strong tip. The one-armed man, nursing a Bud at the end of the bar, rambling on about a speeding ticket. What are the sources of movement and light within a dark bar on a Saturday afternoon? The flicker of the golf tournament on television. The door to the street, and to the daylight, flopping open then shut. The scattering of pool balls. The bartender wiping the counter. Each of these elements of scene is a potential reaction for the character. The brother might wince at the light from outside. He might jump at the snap break on the pool table or lift his hands so the bartender can pass through with his rag. These are all movements incidental to place. They don't indicate attitude or character. Anyone would do the same thing. Still, movements like this tend to get overlooked by the writer struggling with a dialogue. The incidental gesture can be used to fill a pause, or to define a silence too. You have to learn to trust these gestures within dialogue, just as you would the spoken word.

Place

Notice how the incidental gesture rises out of the circumstance or setting of a given dialogue. Place can, and should, be part of a dialogue. We cannot stop the interruptions of the world, and just as we interact with the world (as in the incidental gesture), so too does it interact with us. *Allow the setting to become part of your dialogue.* This is another means of quieting a dialogue, since it takes the word right out of the speaker's mouth.

At the start of Albert Camus' *The Stranger*, the narrator's mother has died. He travels to the home where she lived to settle her affairs. At one point, he finds himself in a room with the caretaker of the home, looking at his mother's casket. They speak, but the conversation is as much between the narrator and the place as it is between the two men left there.

> When she'd gone the caretaker said, "I'll leave you alone." I don't know what kind of gesture I made, but he stayed where he was, behind me. Having this presence beating down my neck was starting to annoy me. The room was filled with beautiful late-afternoon sunlight. Two hornets were buzzing against the glass roof. I could feel myself getting sleepy. Without turning around, I said to the caretaker, "Have you been here long?" Right away he answered, "Five-years"—as if he'd been waiting all along for me to ask.
>
> After that he did a lot of talking.

The room is largely quiet, but the tension is palpable—between the two men, between the narrator and his world—and it is reflected in the details of the room, which speak to him as loud as any voice. Those hornets! Every time I see a hornet inside my house, bobbing along the ceiling toward escape, I think of that conversation and the light shining through that glass ceiling. Still, looking at the passage again, I see that the conversation itself is quite slight. Its effect is a matter of positioning the characters just so and allowing the world to speak in their silence.

Sherwood Anderson's "The Egg" is a son's chronicle of his father's failed attempts at being an entrepreneur and showman. His father, a failed chicken farmer, buys a tiny restaurant near a railroad station in a rural part of Ohio. He wants the spot to be remarkable, something memorable to passersby, so that people will spread the word. He lays out baskets of eggs and lines the shelves with the genetic oddities collected in his days on the chicken farm. He attempts to perform for the customers as they wait for the trains. In the story's one section of dialogue, we hear the father's failed routine as he tries it out on a customer.

> . . . he did not know what to do with his hands. He thrust one of them nervously over the counter and shook hands with Joe Kane. "How-de-do," he said. Joe Kane put his newspaper down and stared at him. Father's eye lighted on the basket of eggs that sat on the counter and he began to talk. "Well," he began hesitatingly, "well, you have heard of Christopher Columbus, eh?" He seemed to be angry. "That Christopher Columbus was a cheat," he declared emphatically. "He talked of making an egg stand on its end. He talked, he did, and then he went and broke the end of the egg."
>
> My father seemed to his visitor to be beside himself at the duplicity of Christopher Columbus. He muttered and swore. He declared it was wrong to teach children that Christopher Columbus was a great man when, after all, he cheated at the critical moment. He had declared that he would make an egg stand on end and then when his bluff had been called he had done a trick. Still grumbling at Columbus, father took an egg down from the basket on the counter and began to walk up and down. He rolled the egg between the palms of his hands. He smiled genially. He began to mumble words regarding the effect to be produced on an egg by the electricity that comes out

of the human body. He declared that without breaking its shell and by virtue of rolling it back and forth in his hands he could stand the egg on its end. He explained that the warmth of his hands and the gentle rolling movement he gave the egg created a new center of gravity, and Joe Kane was mildly interested. "I have handled thousands of eggs," father said. "No one knows more about eggs than I do."

He stood the egg on the counter and it fell on its side. He tried the trick again and again, each time rolling the egg between the palms of his hands and saying words regarding the wonders of electricity and the laws of gravity. When after half an hour's effort he did succeed in making the egg stand for a moment he looked up to find that his visitor was no longer watching.

Although the scene involves a lot of talking, notice how little of it the reader actually hears. Anderson slowly drops the father's words as the scene progresses. The customer never speaks. Gesture and the details of place combine to take the place of words. The tone of the narration does the work of the customer's reaction. The primary audience—the customer Joe Kane—is accosted by the father's act, probably overwhelmed by his words, yet the secondary audience is able to see the whole failure in a broader, more irrefutable light, without reading every single word of the act. This is a circumstance where a man is trying to be chatty, yet the purposes of the story are better served by concentrating on the balance of monologue, physical expression and scene.

QUIETING THE NARRATOR

Up to now we've seen the silence that accompanies pauses and breaks in conversation. We've further seen that these silences need not be "quiet" in the traditional sense. The tools of narrative ask the writer to fill them with the squeaks, groans and whistles of everyday life. This is what a narrator does. He fills in; he sharpens; he shapes. But just as you have to quiet characters from time to time, so that dialogue is sharp and well chosen, you have to understand that there are moments in a story when a dialogue can take over. When the words of the characters will suffice. In these moments the writer must quiet the narrator and resist the urge to fill.

Edmund White's masterful memoir, *A Boy's Own Story*, is a chronicle of the author's coming-of-age and coming out of the closet in the
1950s. Like most nonfiction, it relies upon the elements of fiction for
the shape and tone of the story. The truth is, it is as much a novel
as most novels hope to be. In one scene, the high-school-aged
protagonist returns home from one of his first and only dates with a
woman. It went well and, torn between his emergent homosexuality
and the desire to make his family happy, he feels some hope that he
might be able to transform himself into an upstanding heterosexual,
despite his deeper realization of who he is. Upon returning home, he
finds his sleepy mother wants to hear how the date went. The dialogue
breaks about every rule I've suggested to you so far. (The long blank
space in the middle of the dialogue appears to indicate an expletive.)

> When I got home my mother was in bed with the lights out.
> "Honey?"
> "Yes?"
> "Come in and talk to me."
> "Okay," I said.
> "Rub my back, okay?"
> "Okay," I said. I sat on the bed beside her. She smelled of
> bourbon.
> "How was your date?"
> "Terrific! I never had such a good time."
> "How nice. Is she a nice girl?"
> "Better than that. She's charming and sophisticated and
> intelligent."
> "You're home earlier than I expected. Not so hard. Rub
> gently. You bruiser. I'm going to call you that: Bruiser. Is she
> playful? Is she like me? Does she say cute things?"
> "Not an egghead, but she's dignified. She's straightforward.
> She says what she means."
> "I think girls should be playful. That doesn't mean dishonest.
> I'm playful."
> "_____"
> "Well, I am. Do you think she likes you?"
> "How can I tell? It was just a first date." My fingers lightly
> stroked her neck to either side of her spine. "I doubt if she'll
> want to see me again. Why should she?"

"But why not? You're handsome and intelligent."

"Handsome! With these big nostrils?"

"Oh that's just your sister. She's so frustrated she has to pick on you. There's nothing wrong with your nostrils. At least I don't see anything wrong. Of course, I know you too well. If you like, we could consult a nose doctor." A long pause. "Nostrils . . . Do people generally dwell on them? I mean, do people think about them a lot?" Small, high voice: "Are mine okay?"

A hopeless silence.

Study this dialogue out of the context of Edmund White's book and you might decide that it's a limpid ramble. All that meaningless chatter! Too many unnecessary exchanges. Too many trivialities. The writer uses dialogue exchanges solely to touch on plot issues. You might think I'd be pulling my hair out when I read something like this. To this I say, pay attention to the rule that questions the need for all rules, then study what the dialogue actually does. It's a sort of story unto itself.

It opens with an exchange of chatter, sure. But look how completely stripped down the scene is. The truth is, there is little attempt to set the scene, no description of the mother except for the smell of bourbon and the mention of her spine (two small, intriguing details). So the dynamic between mother and son exists on solely this plain of conversational niceties. Only when he agrees to rub her back does the physical circumstance come into play in some manner. Now look at the direction of the dialogue. The mother's character drives the conversation from the start. With each exchange, it presses closer in on her needs, rather than on her son's. ("Rub my back, okay?" "Is she like me?" "Are [my nostrils] okay?") On its own, each is a relatively benign question. But around these words, the bare and largely silent scene accentuates the narrator's isolation within this house, this family and this world. There's little movement and no sense of detail. Not much is revealed in the words themselves. Rather the silence of the scene, clearly reflected in the dearth of narrative detail and stated directly in the closing line, dominates. This pervading silence is as indicative as any single line. The story within the dialogue is of a boy cut off from any real sense of connection by a mother who can see little except herself. This thread can be seen clearly even here, out of context, taken as a story in itself.

Is that enough to make a successful story, that little summary? Surely not. My point is *not* that an effective dialogue can be a story unto itself. Rather, I want you to see that a good dialogue relies on many of the same principles of the larger story in which it appears. Character. Tension. Scene. They're all present. Even dialogue where the narration is toned down. In this case, these things work not so much for the words on the page as for the silence that replaces them.

Quieting a Character

Silence takes many forms. For the writer, cognizant of every force working within the story, it is often a matter of "turning down the knob" on one of those elements. Whereas, in the above example, White pares away the element of scene and minimizes the narrative consciousness, many writers silence one member of a dialogue in order to make the words of the other resonate on the page. In the following example from John Cheever's "Goodbye, My Brother," the narrator and his brother examine the outside of their family's vacation house. While we hear the brother, Lawrence, in conversation, the narrator is conspicuously silent. That part of the character's voice is turned down, but notice how memory and narrative consciousness rise up to fill his silence.

> He pointed out to me, at the base of each row of shingles, a faint blue line of carpenter's chalk. "That house is about twenty-two years old," he said. "These shingles are about two hundred years old. Dad must have bought shingles from all the farms around here when he built the place, to make it look venerable. You can still see the carpenter's chalk put down where the antiques were nailed into place."
>
> It was true about the shingles, although I had forgotten it. When the house was built, our father, or his architect, had ordered it covered with lichen and weather-beaten shingles. I didn't follow Lawrence's reasons for thinking this was scandalous.
>
> "And look at these doors," Lawrence said. "Look at these doors and window frames." I followed him over to a big Dutch door that opened onto the terrace and looked at it. It was a relatively new door, but someone had worked hard to conceal its newness. The surface had been deeply scored with some metal implement, and the white paint had been rubbed into

the incisions to imitate brine, lichen and weather rot. "Imagine spending thousands of dollars to make a sound house look like a wreck," Lawrence said. "Imagine the frame of mind this implies. Imagine wanting to live so much in the past that you'll pay men carpenter's wages to disfigure your front door." Then I remembered Lawrence's sensitivity to time and his sentiments and opinions about our feelings for the past. I had heard him say, years ago, that we and our friends and our part of the nation, finding ourselves unable to cope with our problems of the present, had, like a wretched adult, turned back to what we supposed was a happier and simpler time, and that our taste for reconstruction and candlelight was a measure of this irremediable failure. The faint blue line of chalk had reminded him of these ideas. . . .

The narrator's silence is understandable and appropriate. It's clear that Lawrence isn't listening. The literal conversation has dropped away. Were the writer a mere tape recorder in a conversation of this length, we would surely hear, or see, the narrator make some response—some question to hasten things along, a nod of assent, a grunt even. But Cheever makes no attempts to duplicate, or even indicate, the narrator's responses. Meanwhile, the past rises up in the narrator's conscious, even as the brother regales the father for hiding in the past. Thus the contrary forces at work in the house, old and new, past and present, become part of the tension of the scene. These tensions are brought to a head when the family comes in from the tennis court.

It's hardly a quiet dialogue. Lawrence is venting and the past is roaring up in the narrator's mind. The physical world is shining through. But it is a dialogue, even though one person does not speak. The narrator is no less a part of the dialogue because he is silent. The narrative voice takes over and goes further into the questions that the story raises. Resisting the urge to respond in dialogue, to engage the narrator with the spoken word, is part of the muscle Cheever displays in his dialogue. It is a demonstration of control.

A WORD ON CONTROL

It takes strength to be silent. It takes control. Choosing when to stop, when to mute, when to strip away is a key to writing dialogue that is well integrated with your fiction. As we've seen, silence is often an answer. Choose it, surprise yourself with it, rely on it. But never simply fall back on it because you are tired of a scene or an exchange. It is not a tool for the lazy. It must become an element of your language, a choice made from *within* a dialogue rather than as a means of getting out of one. Use silence to express, rather than to evade, and it will serve better than any thesaurus.

EXERCISES

1. Give bubble talk a try. Without reading them closely, collect the Sunday comics for a few weeks. Then ask a friend to "white out" the dialogue bubbles. Now, after examining each strip for the tone of the illustration and the accompanying gesture, create convincing dialogue. The words should accompany the pictures and fit within the bubbles. After a while, try to work against the meaning of the pictures. Let the words grate against the form of the bubble. Now turn this wit back onto your fiction, removing it from the bubbles and drawing the scene in words.

2. Set up a scene in which two people are arguing. You choose the argument. If you can't think of one, use the story of the two brothers in the bar. (Surely you can do better.) Write a two-page scene in which the two argue, but write it so the reader can only hear one of them. Silence the other, having him narrate the dialogue. We should never hear his words within the dialogue. This dialogue can become a rich tissue of memory, gesture and scene. Lean on these elements while writing it.

3. Write a list of the particular gestures of your friends. This will involve carrying your spiral for a few days. Watch your buddies closely. Watch their hands, notice the way they walk, their stance when talking to others. List three particular gestures for each friend, or more if you can get them. Show the list around. See if people recognize their quirks. Save the list and refer to it while writing dialogue. It will be a rich source for many stories.

4. Draw a line down the middle of a page. At the top of one column, write the word "Place," and at the top of the other, write "Gesture." Now spend several days charting your own incidental gestures. Don't

watch for peculiarities so much as for the way you move in certain spaces. Here's a sample list.

Place	Gesture
Laundromat	Sitting cross-legged on washer
	Flipping comic book with pinkie
At red light	Pounding steering wheel with palm

This sort of list can be a rich and important source of detail for your stories.

5. Quiet the narrator. Write a back-and-forth narrative (in which the first character speaks, followed immediately by the other, followed immediately by the first character and so on), but don't put in any of the details of the physical world. Use a simple "he said," "she said" format, but remember, no locations, no "props," no background. The scene should involve something urgent, but not dangerous, so the characters feel compelled to speak (such as have an argument), but not so urgent they are reacting to the world around them (not a rainstorm). After ten exchanges, allow yourself one, well-chosen physical detail within the dialogue and no more. Press the dialogue to an appropriate moment of silence. Once finished, examine. Are the elements of story there? What's missing? How can you press that into the exchange without employing the narrative voice? Do it.

SIX

RADIO, TV, MOVIES

SEEING, LISTENING, READING

All my life the people around me have been dancing a strange two-step with radio, TV and the movies. I have friends who never listen to the radio, because they consider talk radio déclassé or they like picking their own music. I have another set of friends that never watches television, for the usual set of reasons: too mindless, too predictable, bland writing, fuzzy sentiments. Many people I know share the same feelings about movies, particularly commercial ones, which tend to be written and rewritten so often they become a mish-mash of homogenized ideas. I accept all of that as the general truth.

It is tempting to say to the fiction writer, "Avoid radio! Turn off the television! Reject 'Hollywood' movies!" It's pretty easy for me to see what's wrong with all three of these vehicles. But, quite frankly, I do "connect" with all three. I listen to radio, I watch television and I go to movies. To say that I get nothing from them, no sense of the way language does and doesn't work, would be a lie. I love good writing, and despite what you may have heard, there's a lot of it going on in these media. What this chapter does is ask you to rethink the way you use them. Instead of listening to the radio, I want you to *see* it. Don't watch television, *listen* to it. Don't just go to the movies, *read* them. You'll find lots of the bad, some of the good and a few places to start turning the lessons into good fiction.

EYES CLOSED

When there's a decent AM radio station on in the background, I enjoy almost everything about a long drive. I like the cup of coffee in the crappy cup in the drink holder. I like the pace of the interstate. I like the whine and pop of the AM dial, better than the filtered hiss of FM. The less music, the better. I go AM because I listen for talk. I like the stray phrases I catch—the cloying sentiment of the religious channels, the indignant chiding of the talk-show hosts, even the heavily compressed scripts of the commercials, where words are squeezed into spaces too tight for their own good.

I like to think of this as training I received from my mother, who, as a child of the '40s, learned to love stories as much through listening to the radio as through reading books. And while there's very little dramatic or comedic radio on the air these days (and what little there is, is overly clever and completely content with vamping the real stuff), I listen for the same things I listen for in a restaurant, at the park or on a subway car. Paul Harvey is neither Amos nor Andy, and Dr. Laura Schlessinger is not the Phantom, but they have personality, character, their own personas, and they're transmitted by words as much as by the airwaves. As always, I listen for words.

If you've read this far, you know I have faith in listening. So it makes sense that I'd like radio. Listening is the way we read the world. You can "view" the world if you want, but for the writer, listening teaches as much or more. The act of listening itself is as close to reading as you can get without actually picking up a book. Unlike viewing— watching a movie or gazing at the television—listening is not entirely passive. You have to listen hard; you have to fight to interpret. As a writer, you have to separate and see the language, ignoring much in the process. So close your eyes. Listen.

In old radio programs, sound effects filled the silences. Doors slammed. Keys rattled. Cars started. Windows broke. Music rose and fell toward the end of each act. Still, dialogue propelled the story, linked it to the week before and drew the audience in, bent on making them want more. Its intent was never to sound "realistic." My mother once told me about listening to the radio in the 1940s: "My father and I stared at anything at all. The bookshelf. The window. It hardly mattered. We listened so hard that we could see the stories unfolding."

Do yourself a favor and go to the library and borrow a tape of an old radio program, a serial drama preferably, such as "The Phantom." Train yourself to see the action, even if it's only hinted at and never explained. The formula is strangely like fiction. We can't explain, or describe, every action in short stories. A woman gets up to leave, and we say, "She got up and left." Nothing unfair about that description; nothing complete about it either. This is a good lesson to apply to dialogue too. You can't include everything.

At times, old radio dialogue tries hard to do just that, to include everything. What's compelling about the best dialogue you hear on old radio shows is how it keeps us within the story, shows us what grew out of last week and points out where the story is moving toward now. While any one line may sound realistic, that is, it may sound like the diction and syntax of the time, taken as a pattern, much of the dialogue is simply devoted to dealing with the limitations of the show—the medium itself, radio, and the time allotted. It is anything but realistic. Say our radio show begins in the lobby of a hotel.

> "Baron Wilberstaff! Here in London! I thought I saw the last of
> you on Mount Komo!"

What's indicated there? A name. A context. A tension. Bang! The elements of story are in place. Rarely does the fiction writer need to move this quickly. Even more rarely should he.

You have to recognize that. And listening to old radio, you are sure to notice these patterns, to think of them perhaps as clumsy and manipulative. Who would listen to that now? What were these people thinking of? First off, recognize what makes this stuff work. Timing, drama, suspense. People listened because they cared. Characters grew from week to week, from night to night, as did story lines. Recognize too how difficult and limiting the form is. On radio when someone brandishes a gun, there is no sound that can be reproduced. The dialogue must carry the day: "Hank! What are you doing with that gun?" "I've had it, I tell you!"

Finally, recognize that this is a commercially driven endeavor. The writers are dealing with two audiences: the national audience and the sponsors, who demand that listeners keep listening. If the dialogue sounds clumsy, you can begin to see why. These writers were limited by time in a way that fiction writers almost never are. Time is the ultimate tool for the fiction writer. In fiction, a short dialogue can be spun out over pages, by modulating it. A long dialogue can be compressed into a few key lines, or the consciousness of the narration can discuss the tension behind the dialogue even as it happens. Radio has to put everything out front. Compare these two examples.

Fictional Treatment

Jenny broke the vase. The key had been hidden there for weeks, and now there it was on the ground between us like a little brass mushroom. Neither of us moved to touch it. Outside Magliori was taking an ax to the old chicken. I could hear his feet kicking though the dust as he chopped.

"Sorry," she said. "Sorry." And she turned back to the window as if nothing had been revealed.

Radio Treatment

SOUND: A VASE DROPS

> HENRY
> Jenny, you dropped the vase.

> JENNY
> Clumsy! I'm sorry.

SOUND: A KEY FALLS TO THE FLOOR

> JENNY
> What's that?

> HENRY
> It's a key.

> JENNY
> What is it a key to?

> HENRY
> I think we both know.

SOUND: CHOPPING

> JENNY
> Sorry, sorry.

The fictional treatment works better, because so much less is laid on the line with every word. The details of the world set the tone in the fictional piece. In the radio treatment, they merely inch the plot line along.

So why listen to it? Inside the greater pattern of the whole script are the smaller patterns of drama, and they are entirely driven by the characters' words. Listen carefully and you'll pick up on the subtle elements of diction and syntax particular to a given culture and era. Listen carefully and you'll find the potent line buried in the deepest melodrama. These words are material. But concentrate on *seeing* the story and you are using the dialogue the way a reader can in a well-written story. You are crafting a vision from words—spoken words here, on the radio—just the way a reader will craft her vision of your fictional world with words—written words, your words. *See the story.* That's what your reader is doing too. You have to pick and choose. Listen to train yourself to know when enough is enough. Listen for the way the actor's tone of voice is dictated by the writer's choice of words.

You have to select, not imitate. You don't want your dialogue to sound like it came off an old radio show. (Well, I suppose there are stories in which that is *exactly* what you want, but then my advice is still the same: Listen to a lot of them. Don't sell them short.) And for the same reasons, I think you don't want your fiction to sound like television writing. As a teacher, I see this happening all the time. As a writer, as a citizen of the world, I try to fight against it as much as and as best I can. Does that mean you can't watch television and learn?

LISTENING TO TV
You watch television. You know you do. It's late, it's after work or school or it's the middle of the night and there you are grabbing the remote, flipping around, then settling, for some reason, into a rerun of *Get Smart*. You slide back in the couch, adjust your pillow. You don't even glance at the clock. You settle in for a while. Or perhaps you're high-brow, you pick your shows wisely, and there you are, watching that stilted adaptation of "Brideshead Revisited" for the third time. Either way, that's you, in front of the television. I'm not saying you're necessarily some five-hour-a-day statistic either. But, come on, TV happens.

Now get over yourself. Television can be crap, you heard right, but television is not always full-bore bad. As a teacher I see too many stories that ape the shape and structure of poor television, but my point isn't that you should or shouldn't be watching television, it's that you do watch it, or you have watched it or you will and that you have to be aware of what it can do. What I tell my fiction writers is *when you watch, be sure you're watching out. Listen.*

Ask yourself some questions about what you're watching: What do you hate about lousy television shows? Easy resolutions? Plot inconsistencies? The joke-a-minute pace? The canned laughter? All good bones of contention if you ask me. So watch the last five minutes of a bad show, say *The Brady Bunch.* Most of the problems of the show are taken care of by some lousy synopsis of conflict and statement of a common lesson, usually delivered by one of the parents. This sort of shallow dialogue is self-serving, and I'm going to warn you against it at every turn. This stuff sounds bad because there's no reason for it. In the context of our lives, we rarely have to summarize where we stand at a given moment, even a moment of tension.

"Wow. Tax time is right around the corner and I've let my addiction to antianxiety medicine allow me to become blasé about my fiscal obligations to the government."

Nor do we tend to offer clear, concise resolutions for people, not even fellow Bradys, without some time for reflection.

"Sometimes when we grab the bull by the horns, we take care of two birds with one stone. When you toss aside that Ativan, Bobby, I'm sure those 1040EZ forms won't seem quite so daunting. Come on, let me give you a hand. We'd better hurry! This might be the final year for the earned income tax credit!"

But you can't hate the television show simply for doing what it has to. Consider what the writers are up against. There's a commercial coming; the credits are about to roll. Time is the issue! Look at another show, one that holds the same basic shape of *The Brady Bunch,* a family dealing with certain key turmoils (and there are dozens of them). Pick a well-written show, *Roseanne,* for instance. Even there, the moments of synopsis are present, if cleverly hidden in the last five minutes of every show. Dan hitches his belt and sighs. Or Rosie sits at the kitchen table with a magazine. At some point, a switch is hit and, for just a moment, they are telling us what they have learned, or what has changed, or where they will go from here.

This is the most dangerous moment for a fiction writer to echo. Think about it. On the television show, the setting makes little difference. The placement of the resolution within plot is predictable.

It's a simple reminder of a theme, of the lesson of the show. That's part of selling the show. In fiction, the "lesson" need not be stated; in truth, it ought not to be. The resolution is part of the art of the story. It touches every moment in the story that precedes it.

Yet, in television, the lesson must be stated. Look at resolutions in television. The moment itself is hardly important. Listen for it. I'm telling you it happens in every show, from *Matlock* to *Friends*, from *I Dream of Jeannie* to *Twin Peaks*. The statement is so explicit it's clear the character's words are being used by the writer as a reminder to the audience and for nothing else. We accept this as part of the form. That's television. What makes shows such as *Roseanne* better than most is that true resolution is rarely delivered by anyone, let alone dished up every episode like a hefty plate of the Brady's pork chops and applesauce.

It seems that in television, everything must be stated. The dialogue must be used at some point as a tool of the writer, the sponsor, the network, whoever. Blindfold yourself and *listen* to television. You won't need to peek. Action rarely takes the place of words. Gesture is given over to the actors, seen as a mere part of interpretation. Meaning must become explicit in the time allotted. The writer must make everything digestible, use his words in a measured, formulated sense. The fiction writer is free of these sorts of aesthetic handicaps.

What you learn from listening to television is the ability to experience things self-consciously. Once you've studied literary dialogue for a long time, the lack of pretense in television may seem somehow refreshing. Still you have to set rules for yourself. Understand what you don't have to do (you don't need easy resolutions!) and you will be able to see what you must do (complexity is your friend). Some rules, from listening to television.

Don't rush. No need to make your dialogue do the work of closure. For you, the fiction writer, the commercial isn't coming up. There are few long speeches in commercial television. No monologues in any real sense of the word. That's because television breaks meaning into small bites, easily digested, to make the message clearer. When you sit there, blindfolded, you'll be amazed at how quickly people talk and how little real silence there is. This should translate in your fiction to *don't rush*.

Leave some space. Resist the urge to put it all in words. On television, the characters often say things that just happened ("Who was that on the phone?" "That rock almost killed you! One step closer to the edge and wham!").

Resist exposition. Television writers have viewers dropping in at many different moments of the show. One of the things the creators must do is allow each line of dialogue to have some capacity as a piece of setup, or as exposition. Exposition has a place in stories of course, but it ought not to leak into the dialogue time and again.

Brady-ized Dialogue

I often see moments in early drafts of stories where dialogue is used to stretch scenes. There's really no need for this. There are too many things—sounds, thoughts, distant trains—that ought to fill up the lulls within a story. When you start to use words in that way, you are merely filling the emptiness with empty moments. I think a lot of this trouble comes from television, which by nature and necessity has few moments of real silence. Movies are different (and we'll touch on this later), but in television the camera is rarely off the character, and even more rare are moments when that character is allowed to be silent or still. Most programs are an endless string of chatter. When this effect slips into a written dialogue, I say the dialogue has been Brady-ized—reminiscent of a conversation from the old *Brady Bunch* show.

As a teacher I see a lot of Brady-ized dialogue. I can drum it up pretty quickly, because I see the characteristics even in fairly brief exchanges. The key here is that each line has a purpose in the propulsion of plot, conflict and theme. There's generally little attention to timing, music or mystery, three great keys to character within short fiction. While reading the following example, write down the calculated effect of each exchange. I won't set up the scene with any more than a location.

"Man," he wondered aloud, "when is Sharon getting home?"

"What's that, Bill?" said Lily, looking up from her knitting.

"I was just wondering when Sharon is going to get back," he said.

"Don't worry so much, Bill," she said. "You'll know soon enough."

"You're right, Lily. It's just a checkup after all."

"Right."

"It's just . . ."

"Just what?"

"Well, I'm worried that she won't tell the doctor the whole story."

"You mean . . ."

"Yes, I mean our . . . history."

"Oh, Bill, you don't think she would hold back?"

"Not intentionally. Sharon is an honest person. I'm just worried that she might leave something out."

"Well," Lily said, as she looked out the window, "now you've got me worried."

"You and me both," Mike said.

You might be asking yourself, Does he think that's good television dialogue? The answer is no. I think that's Brady-ized dialogue in that each character pulls the other along. Every line of dialogue invites, virtually demands, the next. There is no rhythm or pace or surprise. It's guilty of some of the same flaws that bad television writing falls prey to, for whatever reason, good or bad, the sort of stuff that creeps into the worst daytime television writing and the weakest television movies. Think of the list of rules gleaned from listening to television. This dialogue breaks them all: It rushes the tension forward, it leaves no room for silence, it is heavily expository. Every line in the exchange is a servant to plot and nothing more. There isn't a drop of character or place. It's chock full of reminders and rehashes. While you can sense a story all around it (maybe not a good one, but a story nonetheless), this is a dialogue that doesn't serve the heart of the story—unless that heart is a vault of dim-witted, ironic posturing. Check out the way I chart this mess.

"Man," he wondered aloud, "when is Sharon getting home?"   *(establishes tension)*

"What's that, Bill?" said Lily, looking up from her knitting.   *(reminder of name, simple character establishing activity)*

"I was just wondering when Sharon is going to get back," he said.	*(repeats question in case audience missed it)*
"Don't worry so much, Bill," she said. "You'll know soon enough."	*(reminds audience of item frame)*
"You're right, Lily. It's just a checkup after all."	*(increases tension)*
"Right."	*(aimless chatter)*
"It's just . . ."	*(attempt to increase tension again)*
"Just what?"	*(pointless interruption)*
"Well, I'm worried that she won't tell the doctor the whole story."	*(holding back information from audience)*
"You mean . . ."	*(character is a pure sounding board at this point)*
"Yes, I mean our . . . history."	*(tension is revealed slightly more)*
"Oh, Bill, you don't think she would hold back?"	*(rehash/sounding board to clarify tension)*
"Not intentionally. Sharon is an honest person. I'm just worried that she might leave something out."	*(explanation/exposition)*
"Well," Lily said, as she looked out the window, "now you've got me worried."	*(tension shifts slightly to Lily)*
"You and me both," Mike said.	*(tension has been restated three times, without being clarified)*

There's not much I can do if you like that. That is *not* how people sound. That is the way television sometimes sounds. If it sounds like that to you more than once a week, turn it off! (There, I did give you a hard-and-fast rule after all.) Also, *don't chart your own character's dialogue.* There are a lot of books on screenwriting and television writing that claim every line of dialogue should have a purpose. That is lockstep thinking. Plain and simple, in any medium, good dialogue sounds like people talking. They may be intensely witty; they may be evil; they may be a widowed architect with three sons who marries a widow with three daughters, all of them with "hair of gold, like their mother." But they should sound like people talking. So don't chart. It makes you too aware of purpose, of direction, and forces an element of calculation into the words of your characters. Your calculation, not theirs.

If you do chart your dialogue, think of it as a party trick and nothing more. People do not constantly invite one another to "deliver" the next line. Not in fiction, not in life. In fiction writing, you are just mowing down the story for the reader when you engage your characters in dialogue that simply serves to propel the plot line. Okay, I've changed my mind again, chart it if you want. But if it can be clearly charted, you might as well throw it out and start over.

Good Television

So what's to like about television? I've just gone on a harangue about bad television, but there are skills you can learn from watching television: economy, accommodation and timing.

Economy refers to the need to be measured and clear, to take two or three story lines through a relatively short written space. Watch an episode of *Seinfeld*, for instance. In a good one, there are four story lines going through the text of the show at once. Each character carries one subsequent line of conflict from a gathering in the central location into a series of individual scenes, which play out the string. This blends dialogue into the pacing and structure of the show. On this show, tag lines are used to call up the same laugh over and over again; it works too. The lesson to take into your fiction writing is to learn to pinch your language to a minimum, to think of fewer words as being capable of doing more.

Accommodation refers to accommodating the needs of the form and to the fact that many shows have more than one writer, as well as an actor taking up the writer's words. Writers rely on actors for reaction shots, for reliable delivery, for their ability to use the scene around them in some creative fashion. Here, the element to take to your fiction is to remind yourself that everything does not have to be done with the spoken word.

Timing is often in the hands of the actors, but without the scripts, there would be tons of tiresome improvisation. Good timing in the written language is the first step to good timing on the small screen. Watch "The Dick Van Dyke Show". The exchanges in the office are fine examples of the complex effect of layering dialogue, of having several people speak at once. Here, it might be helpful to tape and script out an exchange or two. You'll be surprised at how clipped the dialogue seems on the page. Notice how often people repeat the last thing they heard. It gets laughs. Again, these are reminders that the writer is leaving room for delivery (accommodation) while at the same time working within the confines of the form (economy).

In most television writing, you'll see some evidence of one of these factors. In good television writing, you'll see all three. How do you use this in fiction?

Be aware of the pattern of dialogue. Use repetition. On television, a character will often repeat the last thing another character says, merely to string out the laugh. But sometimes these patterns of repetition are what make the laugh. The language can be fun. Remember, you don't always have to explain.

Watch for what you *don't* have to do. On television, the scene is often the background of the story. Sometimes the words people speak can be the story. Let the words deliver themselves. Avoid adverbs on the end of dialogue tags, as this just becomes a way of defining delivery. If the words are right, the reader will hear them without worrying about the delivery.

Don't sequence scenes around dialogue. Story lines on bad television often begin with someone arriving—coming home from school, walking into the kitchen, returning from the grocery store—or end with someone leaving, followed by a reaction shot. Again, these are functions of form. The writer is allowing the story to open at the moment, reminding the audience of the new start. It's clumsy and trite, and generally sells the audience short. It's one of the parts of the formula that often gets transposed onto otherwise good stories. A dialogue, like a scene, does not need to take us from entry to exit.

Good television, like good fiction, works to create variations: ending dialogues without stretching the text, without people straining to say good-bye or walking out; opening stories in the middle of things. Either case is an example of how television writers are working to keep the character's words from defining the sense of opening and closure of story and scene.

READING MOVIES

Aren't movies a whole lot better than television? To my mind that's like asking: Aren't bagels better than donuts? Same basic shape, similar function, completely different taste and texture. Bagels are better for you, but sometimes you want a donut. On the other hand, the well-dressed bagel can be a meal, whereas the sugary donut rarely suffices. Eat too many donuts, you get fat. Eat too many bagels and you spend all your time arguing the inane question of who makes the best bagel.

For the fiction writer, movies offer constructive models, a chance to see dialogue—often the sort more related to the shape of fiction—coming out of the mouths of talented actors. There's a reliability to this that is undeniable. Good actors make things work. Good writing is improved by good actors; whereas, bad writing can't be masked by the best efforts of a great actor. I have friends who are actors; I respect their work. I am amazed by it. But I would say straight to their faces: The writing is the thing. Once you've read more than a few screenplays, you start to see they are the tautest, most disciplined pieces of writing in existence. The writer goes to the movies to study. Then he reads the movies to study some more.

It's hard for me to understand why screenplays aren't studied as great literature. It's as if the act of creating the movie, of putting it on celluloid, flipped some switch that took the screenplay itself out of commission. Read the best screenplays of the century—*Mildred Pierce, Chinatown, The Big Sleep, Citizen Kane* (make your own list, but read the ones on it)—and go figure what makes them so different in value from great fiction. Many of the best fiction writers of the last seventy-five years spent some part of their careers writing movies. William Faulkner, Sherwood Anderson, Dorothy Parker, Lillian Hellman wrote them. Today writers such as Paul Auster are doing some of their best work in screenplay form. And many young directors think of themselves as writers first. So what are you? Too good for that lower form? Hey. You're a writer. Writers read. Wouldn't you read candy wrappers if you thought there was a story in it? I sure would. (I just checked a Powerhouse though. No story as of yet.) So if you haven't already, you should read a movie. Not see a movie. Not rent a movie. *Read* one.

And screenplays are hellacious things, designed to suggest rather than determine the interpretation of a scene, to call up the imagination of the reader (primary reader: the producer and director, rather than you or me) to provide a minimal framework upon which the actor (another designated reader) creates character. Look at that—suggestion, imagination, minimalism and character. That stuff is right up the good fiction writer's dialogue alley.

What to Expect When You Read a Movie

Read a good novel and the screenplay of the movie made from it at the same time. Look at specific moments that are common to each. Look, preferably, for a movie like *The Player*, which was adapted by Michael Tolkin from a novel he wrote. As you're reading, try to answer certain key questions: How does the screenwriter work differently to elicit tension from a scene than the novelist would? What does the extra attention to scenic detail, to voice, to internal narration add to the dialogue of the novel? What does the sheer economy and straightforward quality of the screenplay offer the same scene? If we assume the novel is the point of origin, what is lost in translation into screenplay?

If we examine a key scene from Tolkin's *The Player*, we begin to see some answers. *The Player* is the story of Griffin Mill, a top studio executive struggling to save his job in the cutthroat movie business. It's his job to decide which movies get made and which don't for his studio. He is reviled by the writers who "pitch" stories at him throughout the day and envied by those around him. The book, and the movie made from it, is a dark, sardonic look at the world of Hollywood executives. At the start of the story, Mill is receiving anonymous postcards from a disgruntled writer. Caught in the middle of a change of power at work, in danger of losing his job, his standing in the industry, Mill feels threatened by the postcards and paws through his daily planner to find the writer who might be behind the mysterious messages. From the dozens of possibilities, he settles on David

Kahane, with whom he canceled an appointment and never made a follow-up call. He goes to get a look at Kahane, whose idea he can't remember, at a movie theater in Pasadena. Kahane is surprised and somewhat threatened that Mill has tracked him down after all these months. He agrees to have a drink with Mill at a karaoke bar.

The dialogue below is taken from the scene in the bar. It is interesting to compare the novelist's treatment of this scene and the screenwriter's, particularly because in this case the two are one in the same: Michael Tolkin.

"Have you ever been to Japan?" asked Kahane.

"No, actually." Why actually?

"I lived there for a year. I was a foreign exchange student when I was in high school."

"It must have been fun."

"It was. I think about it all the time."

"Have you written about it?"

"No, I told you. You were right, I decided it would have made a good script, but who would care?" No wonder Kahane hated Griffin. The hatred was deserved. He had pitched a story that came from his life, and Griffin had dismissed it. Griffin wanted to defend himself, if the story was so good Kahane should have written it, anyway.

When the waitress brought the drinks, Griffin reached for his wallet for cash instead of a credit card, so Kahane wouldn't think he was generous only with the studio's money, but she wasn't asking for money yet. He fumbled with his wallet and hoped that Kahane hadn't noticed the awkward gesture. Kahane drank his beer and watched the room. Griffin couldn't tell if Kahane also knew that Griffin had forgotten the story. Was he thinking, Why did I let this stranger tell me my life's best story wasn't worth writing about? Kahane turned to him.

"You called my home at seven o'clock. You couldn't have seen the whole movie. You came to the theater looking for me. I called home when I got to the theater. I thought I'd lost my briefcase, but it was in my car. I wanted to let my girlfriend know, so she'd stop looking for it. Why did you call? What are you doing here?"

"I'm apologizing."

"For what? All your shitty movies?"

"I said I'd get back to you."

"If I believed everyone in Hollywood who says that, I'd be crazy."

Now read that comparable scene from the movie. Notice the differences in setting and pace. But notice too how much higher the tension is when it's revealed that Griffin does not remember the idea Kahane had pitched him.

INTERIOR: KARAOKE BAR, NIGHT

GRIFFIN and KAHANE are at a table. There are Asian men in suits, a slew of hostesses and a karaoke machine. A drunk Japanese man holds a microphone and sings.

                    KAHANE
You ever been to Japan?

                    GRIFFIN
Yeah, once, on a location scout with Stephen . . .
Spielberg.

                    KAHANE
I lived there for a year. Student year abroad.

                    GRIFFIN
Great. I wish, I wish I'd done that.

                    KAHANE
I think about it a lot. I'll never forget it.

                    GRIFFIN
You should write about it.

                    KAHANE
I did. Don't you remember?

                    GRIFFIN
What?

The drinks arrive.

                    KAHANE
Aregato. My idea. About an American student who

goes to Japan. That was my pitch. The one you were supposed to get back to me on.

GRIFFIN is confused.

KAHANE

You don't remember, do you?

The song is over. GRIFFIN applauds briefly.

GRIFFIN

Of course, I remember.

KAHANE

You never got back to me.

GRIFFIN

Listen, I was an asshole, all right? It comes with the job. I'm sorry. I really am. I know how angry it must have made you. I'll make it up to you, that's what I'm here for. I'm gonna give you a deal, David. I'm not going to guarantee I'll make the movie, but I'm gonna give you a shot. Let's just stop all this postcard shit, all right? I'm here to say that I would like to start over. Friends?

GRIFFIN offers him his hand, but KAHANE doesn't shake. KAHANE watches him, and finally GRIFFIN puts his hand down without saying a word.

KAHANE

Fuck you, Mill. You're a liar.

GRIFFIN

You're stepping over the line, David.

KAHANE

You didn't come out here to see *The Bicycle Thief.* You came in five minutes before the picture ended. You nearly tripped over my feet. What'd you do, call my house? Speak to the ice queen? You'd like her, Mill. She's a lot like you. All heart. You're on my list, pal, and nothing's going to change that.

KAHANE gets up and walks.

KAHANE
See you in the next reel, asshole.

KAHANE leaves.

It's senseless to compare the dialogues if all you're trying to do is decide which one is better. Again, donuts and bagels. Examine each one to discover differences between the needs of the form. *The Player* is a good book and a fine movie. You decide which you like better. My point here is that as a writer, you should be watching how other writers deal with the same issues that concern you. In dialogue writing, these issues might be pace, believability, tension and tone.

The movie script works faster. It brings the entire meeting full circle within sixteen exchanges. The novel's dialogue might seem more languidly paced, but only by comparison. There, it takes three pages before Kahane reveals his anger and walks out of the bar. Not much time really, in a sense of what a novel is, but in "movie-think" pages equal minutes (literally one page of a screenplay equals one minute of screen time), that scene might take a lifetime. The screenplay is forced to reveal things through words that serve as exposition (Griffin's arrogance and tendency to name-drop is established in the second line; Kahane tells the audience that Griffin can't remember the pitch; the gesture of the handshake, along with the dialogue that precedes it, is a visible statement of Griffin's intent). I've been saying all along that exposition does not belong in dialogue, at least not in large doses. A good screenplay is invaluable in showing the fiction writer models for dealing with issues of exposition.

The dialogue from the novel, which ends in a parking lot outside the bar, in much the same sort of exchange (Griffin's apology, Kahane's angry retort) as the screenplay's treatment of the scene, is more prone to lean on the things that fiction does well. Griffin's character is revealed consistently throughout, in the narrative asides (in which his sympathies, his anger, his fears and his intent are brought into play). Very little of the tension between them, including the key piece—the fact that Griffin is hiding things from Kahane—needs to be stated by the characters themselves. To my mind, this is what makes fiction the superior form. We are able, even in this small snippet from the book, to see Griffin as arrogant, but confused; somewhat mean, but likable. He is a complex character, rife with contradiction, struggling internally—the sort that doesn't populate the screens of many movies. And Tim Robbins, who plays Mill in the movie, struggles to make him stand as more than a bloodless hatchet man. His success is a matter of his work, the director's work, the cinematographer, the editor, the lighting man, the wardrobe guy, the actors around him and dozens of others. My point here is not that it's better or worse; it's more like the words themselves bear less weight than they do in a novel. The words here are about interpretation and pace.

The obligation of the character's words is wholly different in a movie than it is in fiction. They should not be aped blindly, but studied, read and, when appropriate, admired for what they do well.

ANTS AND BEARS

One final word on these people: actors, directors, editors, producers, grips. Think about how they work. They are like a colony of ants. That's how they work. Ants—limitless in their numbers, each performing a task for the benefit of the colony, operating efficiently, with a sense of almost military precision, circling around a generally indifferent queen. Now, I admire ants greatly. But in general ants are

1. everywhere
2. hard to get rid of
3. important to the ecosystem.

That's truly the case with movie people. They are everywhere and our culture tends to champion them. But remember, fiction writers and screen writers alike: *You are the writer.* You are the bear. You work alone. You travel great distances. Bears are messy and dangerous. Bears are scary! You see many things. They—producers and the rest—they are ants. To them, what a bear does is fairly unimportant, though they do eat a bear's scat, so there is something to be said for their relationship. Remember! Bears are bigger, stronger and more awesome than ants (except when taken in toto). Don't get your sense of value from what movies can do. You are the bear! One bear can do so much more than one ant. Bears rock! Ants bring home the dead bees and make sure the tunnels are wide enough. They tend to be rich ants, true. But still—ants.

EXERCISES

1. Stand with another person. Set up a tape recorder on the table between you. Start feeding each other dialogue. "Hi, I'm home" kinda stuff. Do not set anything up. Not circumstance. Not tension. Not setting. Let the dialogue do the work. Each of you should be pretending you are in a television show. Find the tension. Deliver the setups. Hit the punch lines. On the other hand, speak quickly. Don't hesitate. If you give yourself five minutes, can you find a plot line? If so, back up and start over. Compress. Make the improvisation move toward the tension as fast as possible. If you are able to get to the tension faster, then work to compress it even more. Compare the first version, in which you were searching out a plot line, to the last version, in which the plot line was propelling the dialogue. Type them. Which sounds more natural? Examine the ways the tension and conflict are brought to bear more quickly in the final version.

2. Grab your clicker and turn on the box! Watch one channel until you hear one intelligible sentence. Write that down. Now, before you get into the show, change channels and listen again. Pick up another line. Click again. Write until you have ten separate sentences from ten separate channels. Now reread them. If you have time, put them away for a week or two, until you aren't clear which one came from which channel. Then take the list and, using these random lines as triggers, try to craft mini-scenes around each one. Start with the line you overheard. Strip away the original context and use the line as a starting point to build a new one. Work hard to make these news words suit the context and character you create. Even if you are using a line from a commercial for a butcher shop, try to use the line in a way that makes the words sound like someone speaking. Remember, tone is everything.

3. Write a scene from one of your favorite movies. Without reading the scene from the screenplay first, watch a five- to ten-minute section from one of your favorite movies as a piece of fiction. Keep notes. Try to write down what most of the characters say. Now start writing a mini-scene, translating the film into short fiction. Try to make your writing work the same way the movie does, that is, it ought to achieve a comparable tone, the same effects. Create the setting, set up the circumstance, show the characters as you feel appropriate. Now, start

to fill in the original movie dialogue. Use as much of it as possible. Show it to a reader when finished, asking him to mark moments when the dialogue seems contrived or forced. Rewrite, making the characters speak in convincing voices. When finished, look at the differences you have created. These gaps between forms are the heart of the matter when it comes to watching movies as a fiction writer. Try this with television too, and you may find that the gaps are insurmountable.

4. Blindfold yourself and listen to a good movie, for example *Chinatown, Mildred Pierce* or *Bringing Up Baby.* Keep a pad in your lap as you listen, and mark the number of times you hear a line of dialogue that appears to be mostly expository. Now do the same thing with a bad movie (do I have to make suggestions here?). What do you find? Do better movies use less expository dialogue? In what ways? Use specific lines as examples. Now read a story and keep the same count. As you listen to a movie, listen for lines that seem artificial or forced. Do the same thing with a good story. Make the same sorts of comparisons as you did in the first half of this exercise. Take note of how rarely a character *must* speak in fiction and how often they *do* speak in movies. This is another gap you must seek to understand.

SEVEN

USING DIALOGUE TO CREATE STORIES

You've been at the computer for hours, and it all sounds like the same old horse hockey. Your tone is way off. You have no sense of place, and your usual feel for where a character comes from, of his identity, is just plain missing. All writers have been there. You've been there, or in a place like it. The solution: You wait for the next thing you hear. Learn this quirk; put it in your bag of tricks. *Use dialogue as a trigger* for stories.

I go back to my old advice first. Listen. Don't talk. Listen. If you've trained yourself to be a conscious listener, almost any line of over-heard dialogue can make a starting point. I am sitting here at my computer. I know this moment well. It is 10:34 in the morning. Downstairs my two sons are talking with their mom. I can hear snatches of what they say. My older son fell last night and hurt his arm. It is still sore and he's going in for an X ray this afternoon. Some old friends are coming to see us today, just for the day. He is talking nonstop, tense about the arm (as he broke it once already) and unhappy about having to miss our friends' visit. As I said, I can only hear snatches of what they say. So I decide to crowd them a little. I sit at the top of the stairs. I am recording whatever I hear from my son.

Is that good?

When are they coming?

Am I in my seventh year or my sixth?

Swimming

Is that a deal?

How long

Make sure Anna knows
Yes
I fixed it, no I didn't
I almost fixed it
Not a lot, not a lot
No money. No money.
I'm not having orange juice
OK. OK. Anything but that.
Bad Mamma.
No. It's not our table.
Yes.
Baked potatoes. I don't like them.
When are they going to be here?
When? When?
When?

As I said in chapter one, listening is king. If you want to write, you have to have faith in the world around you, particularly in the voices around you. I'm saying that you can use these voices as more than part of the story. Remember to look for the whole. I've said it before: In the voices, in the words around you, whole stories are waiting.

So what's inviting about the above list? First off, recognize that it isn't a treasure trove. I love my son, but he's not out there to give me material for stories. Some of the lines stink. So you have to ignore a certain amount of what's there. I encourage you to ignore the context too. Just look at the words. The next step is to isolate the lines that suggest something to you. The key here is to eliminate character, as well as context. Just use the words. Once they're on the page, they should become suggestions. Once they show you things you haven't seen before—a circumstance, place and person—then expand, tease the story out.

Pick the line "When? When?" and attach it to an anxious six-year-old and it seems pretty explainable. It could be a "When do we get there?" kind of thing, like a long summer vacation drive. That sort of sums it up. *But when a story can be summed up by a line of dialogue, that line of dialogue should be thrown out.* Remember the power of suggestion. What if the line "When? When?" was coming out of the mouth of a doctor, standing in a brightly lit hallway? Or what if it were shouted toward you by an unseen person down a dark alley? Or over the phone, by a nervous liquor store salesman. How am I doing this? I'm literally jumping around to different places where this dialogue might have occurred. I am using dialogue to lead me to place. It doesn't matter which way these are attached. The key is learning that they are and using them that way.

I go on elsewhere about connecting character to dialogue. This is different. This is using dialogue to help you *invent* characters, to find places, to lead you to stories. Find the words that hold an entire story. First, pin the words to the page. Record. Start with these words. Or work toward them in an existing story. Fill the blank spaces with them and see what happens. Let the character come from a new direction and pick them up.

Of all the lines from the above list, these are the ones that I'm fairly interested in.

No. It's not our table.

No money. No money.

Make sure Anna knows

OK. OK. Anything but that.

Why? I think each of them suggests another character. Each of them stands as a piece of a conversation, whereas other lines (such as "Swimming" or "Baked potatoes. I don't like them.") could be the first words of a monologue. They're fine. You may like them better. All lines are good if you can use them. But for me, the best idea is to pull the words toward another person, to implicate and ignite a human circumstance. So I gravitate toward the lines where another person has just spoken or seems to be called on for response.

Once isolated, I tend to write these words by hand on an index card. I tape that card to the top of my computer so I see it each time I come in and sit down to start up. Or I carry it with me through the day, using it to write down phone numbers and shopping lists so I pull the card out at many different times, in many different contexts. Either of these works for me. The computer thing works because then I start up with the line working through my mind. I'm a big believer in mantras. Say the words again and again. So you can hear them without saying them. Frankly this is part of isolating the words from their original source. In this exercise, after I take the words from my son (or whomever), I try to forget he said them. Isolate. Remember: words. You are creating the space, the context around them.

If you're really groping to find character, brainstorming is always a good idea. Write the words on one side of an index card. Read them to yourself. Turn the card over and write down the first thing that comes to mind.

On the front of the card:
"It's not our table."

On the back of the card:
Restaurant

Fairly mundane. But a decent start. Do it again, thinking of a new circumstance. Then again. In each case, make the detail more specific, more contextualized. Yet, remember to make each the start of a new story. Things may clash. Don't worry, you'll be doing lots of crossing out. You can work on consistency later. You are working as fast as you can here, trying to surprise yourself with detail.

On the front of the card:
"It's not our table."

On the back of the card:
Restaurant—outside a trailer—hot night—sticky tablecloth—Jan—moving to a new town—Salt Lake City—a Vietnamese restaurant—a stunning waitress—a monk—

Why these details? Why these names? Well, it's a brainstorm. I'm writing the first thoughts that came to my mind. Where these thoughts came from shouldn't be the point, but I can tell you that I really tried to picture a new setup each time. The first place I chose, the restaurant, had to do with a vision I had of people waiting in the lobby of a beautiful restaurant. I literally did what I asked you to do, that is, turned the card over and came up with a new circumstance, and I was struck by the idea of a person stealing a table from in front of a trailer. I don't know why. I think the line itself—"It's not our table"—suggests a warning, sounds a note of caution. There's no real good reason for either line, but now they suggest starting points, or perhaps two points within the narrative. Then, as I urged you to, I tried to get more specific. I chose Jan, because, frankly, I just watched a movie starring the '70s heartthrob Jan Michael Vincent last night. I wasn't picturing him though. Just a name, a word, a sound. The next lines come from trying to restart the restaurant story. They grow more tied to a particular adventure I had with my brother when I visited him in Salt Lake City. Nothing too marvelous. But when I look back at the list now, I think I begin to see the shape of a single narrative there. Nothing concrete yet. But I have an opening scene, a setting, even a hint of tension.

I'm not sure where the monk could be used (though I'm not sure he *couldn't* be used), but if I were working this brainstorm into a story, I would feel free to cross out the monk detail if it made me feel I was stretching things, pushing the narrative toward the point of absurdity. Cross out. Leave stuff behind. Never let an exercise like this stymie you. Never let any hint stand in your way. If it didn't work then, it wasn't the hint for you, or it was a crappy exercise. This is general advice here. If you get stymied, turn away and start elsewhere. Frankly, I hope that's not happening here. I'm hoping I'm giving you ways around the "blocks" that sometimes come our way. I'm not just generating work here either. I do this stuff. It works for me.

Now brainstorming is wonderful stuff. The best stories in the world probably live inside a writer's notes. But they don't mean much unless they get into a story that gets read. So don't do too much of this. Try it two or three times a day. Just be quick and increasingly precise. Allow your imaginative field of vision to contract or expand as it needs to, but don't force yourself to work on and on. Even if you hate them at first, these notes should grow stronger, and narratives will begin to grow out of them.

Again, the point here is not to be a simple recorder of the world. You have to use your recordings as points of departure. You are training your imagination to use the mundane, generally ignored details of everyday life and cast them into new frames. Ignore, isolate, reinvent, expand. I often tell my students to do this with an image. If something is powerful in a given circumstance—say the sight of a deer in the early morning at the edge of a golf course—then make it more powerful by ignoring that circumstance and using the image somewhere else, by isolating and reinventing it. Imagine the deer at an intersection in the city in the early morning hours. Put the deer at the end of a pier as the first two fishermen of the morning approach. Both of the new images are more surprising, more powerful. It's the same thing with words. Ignore, isolate, reinvent, expand. They can trigger stories. The trick is not to allow them to trigger the easiest story, the one that's right in front of you, but to allow them to help you see new possibilities in the stories right in front of you.

DISCOVERING TENSION

Are any words good enough? Do all words hold a story? Maybe. But you're far smarter than me if you see elaborate stories in every word you hear. You're also probably a very confused person. Get some help. The rest of us should look back at what I've said from the start. You have to ignore. You have to isolate. Put on the word filter. Slash and burn. Cut and run. Whatever. Just get to the core.

But what happens when you like a word or a line and you don't know where to go with it? What happens when you can't sense the momentum within a line or the scene that surrounds it? There are a number of ways to get started.

Add another voice. Let's suppose you're starting with a line from my son's little ramble, say, "I'm not having orange juice." The obvious suggestion is to have a character respond, even to a line that is basically a statement. Forget place, forget time, forget circumstance. There'll be plenty of chances to fix that as you go along. Respond. Allow yourself to be the voice of the other character. Don't be afraid to ask questions. Put the character up against it. But when you are speaking in the character's voice, answer from the developing point of view. When I ask my students to do this, to cross-examine their characters by engaging them, they tell me it's like developing a lie. I disagree. It's rather the opposite. It's developing the truth, discovering it, or uncovering it. So ask questions of your character. Be obvious for a while. Remember you'll be crossing things out wildly.

> 1: I'm not having orange juice.
> 2: Why?
> 1: It hurts my stomach.
> 2: What's wrong with your stomach?
> 1: I have a sensitive stomach.
> 2: Since when?
> 1: Since forever. Since I can remember. Since I was a kid.
> 2: I never knew.
> 1: Well I do.
> 2: I'm sure.
> 1: I'm not having orange juice.

Elsewhere in the book, I talk about the direction of dialogue, about patterns of evasion and questioning. The idea here is to try *not* to be conscious of patterns. Simply hear voices, using one voice to reveal the other. Remember you aren't shaping voices so much as coaxing them forward, asking them to bring their stories along for the ride. My thinking is that you should try it several times, shooting for a different tone in each version. In the above bit, I am trying to find the tension. There's no particular direction. The tone is fairly neutral, but prodding. If I try again, this time shifting the tone to a somewhat angry one, the rhythm and pace shift quickly.

1: I'm not having orange juice.
2: Why?
1: I have a sensitive stomach.
2: Come on.
1: What?
2: Just cut it out.
1: Cut it out? What do you mean?
2: You're whining.
1: Whining? Are you saying I'm a whiner?
2: You got it. You're addicted to medical attention.
1: Meaning what?
2: Meaning nothing.
1: That's not true.
2: Get off it. You're an addict. You can't help yourself.
1: I just don't want any orange juice.
2: Then leave your stomach out of it. You don't want orange juice, don't drink it. But you don't have to tell me all about your insides. We're all a little sick of hearing about your guts all the time.
1: All I was saying . . .
2: I know. I know. No orange juice.

Remember, within these micro dialogues, you have to resist the urge to tell the entire story with the words of the character. *When you're using one character simply to tell the story, rather than as an autonomous voice, that's when you go back and cross out.*

Remember too that *adding tension does not always beef up dialogue.* Some of the best dialogue in the world is somewhat aimless, yet is more artfully revealing, particularly of the dynamic between characters, than any exposition could hope to be. Early on in William

Kennedy's novel *Ironweed*, we meet the book's protagonist, Francis Phelan, an ex-baseball player and out-of-work gravedigger, now a hobo in the Northeast. The book involves his return to his native city, Albany, and his brief visit with the family he left behind years before, after he was responsible for the death of his infant son. In the first pages of the book, before any of this has been revealed, Francis and his sidekick, Rudy, have what appears to be a fairly aimless exchange as they walk by a graveyard where some of Francis' family is buried. It starts after Francis ties his shoe.

> "There's seven deadly sins," Rudy said.
> "Deadly? What do you mean deadly?" Francis said.
> "I mean daily," Rudy said. "Every day."
> "There's only one sin as far as I'm concerned," Francis said.
> "There's prejudice."
> "Oh yeah. Prejudice. Yes."
> "There's envy."
> "Envy. Yeah, yup. That's one."
> "There's lust."
> "Lust, right. Always liked that one."
> "Cowardice."
> "I don't know what you mean. That word I don't know."
> "Cowardice."
> "I don't like the coward word. What're you sayin' about coward?"
> "A coward. He'll cower up. You know what a coward is? He'll run."
> "No, that word I don't know. Francis is no coward. He'll fight anybody. Listen, you know what I like?"
> "What do you like?"
> "Honesty," Francis said.
> "That's another one."

This is a conversation that works in two ways. First time through the book, it helps the readers see the relationship between these two men, allows them to hone in on Francis' edginess with regards to the world of men. Knowing the plot of the book from my summary above, it is possible to see the haunting resonance this conversation has for a man about to revisit his past. Still, keep in mind that the scene begins with a paragraph of Francis tying his ragged shoe and ends when they turn the corner. It is a fairly self-contained scene, seemingly a ramble and little more, and yet as the rest of the novel grows, that dialogue—with its references to sin, prejudice and cowardice—becomes a focal point. Tension does not dominate the conversation. It pervades it. Still, many readers would say they missed that moment entirely, appearing early (page 11) in a 220-plus-page novel. The important thing for you to take away from this is the way the writer is letting the conversation lead him into the themes of the work, the ideas in play within the conflict. The tension is plainly there for the writer. It is also driving Francis, who's fearful of what he'll confront upon his return. Still, taken in the full profile of the novel, set against the many conversations these men have, it appears to be nothing but a conversation between two longtime travelers. And that is the way it should be.

FRAMING TENSION

No matter how holistic you try to be, there are still some techniques you do well and others you do not. Most of my students simply hate approaching similes, whereas I think of them, when done well, as a pleasure both to read and write. I have one friend who hates writing dialogue. It takes her days on end to write one page of the stuff. She avoids it by keeping her characters inside themselves, thinking more than talking. Still, the dialogue she produces is always intriguing and sharp.

I knew another guy several years ago who always started his stories with an argument between two characters. He began with tension and felt it invariably led him to the heart of stories. Thus he forced tension on his characters. He let them run with it, back and forth, then stumbled when it came to a resolution or even a pause, when his gaze was forced outward. He liked the possibilities of argument and little else in his dialogue. The world around his characters continually eluded him. When he started in on scene and place, he often called me for a detail. I'd tell him to look around.

"There's nothing to see. They're in a movie theater," he would say to me. "It's dark. There's no scene."

"How about the movie?"

"What am I supposed to do? Say, 'They were watching *Yentl*'?"

"Be nonspecific. Don't name the movie."

" 'They were watching a movie about rabbis.' Jesus, you're forgetting the conversation entirely."

But I wasn't forgetting the conversation. I was encouraging him to push the conversation outward. I wanted him to use his own particular quirks as a writer (which included a good sense of how to write snappy arguments, his ability to *start* a story with an argument and move from there, instead of moving *toward* an argument at the end of a story) and move from those strengths toward things he hadn't considered. Frankly, my advice was to *get off the conversation, not forget about it, to frame the conversation with a level of detail*, seemingly random, even to the writer, from the scene around it.

I don't see anything wrong with being vague about details of setting. I liked the line about the rabbis. That detail still makes me want to frame a conversation around it.

In the movie theater, two friends are whispering to one another.

> "What am I supposed to do? I'm at a loss."
>
> Someone shushed them from three rows behind. Candy turned and shook her head. "You have to stay strong. Don't let them mess with your kids," she whispered.
>
> "That's just it," he said. "That's the point."
>
> He looked at the screen. It was a movie about rabbis. A woman was serving soup to a man she loved. "Jesus," he said.
>
> "Looks good," Candy said.
>
> "What?"
>
> "Good soup." She kept her eyes on the movie.

I don't know what the conversation is about there, and it's certainly not a starting point for a story. But it may be a scene from within a story: Maybe the man is going through a divorce. Maybe his kids are in some trouble with the law or he owes money to someone dangerous. I chose the line about the kids from one of my notebooks. It was something I overheard on television sometime last spring. I wrote it on the top of a page that ended up going blank. "Don't let them mess with your kids." I just liked the attitude of it (though I had taken it from a sappy television movie). I repeated it three or four times, then wrote it down and forgot about it. I used it here, to start to particularize the tension. Of course here, on the blank slate of this invented scene, it becomes a trigger for a set of circumstances, or for an entire story even (more on this later).

Dialogue Reacts

But the particular direction of this dialogue is elusive. The conversation is not particularly focused. It reacts, both to the subject at hand and to the movie on the screen in front of them. That's life. Rarely are things as focused as we think. The detail of the movie is so peculiar it helps to punctuate the conversation. If I had said they were watching *Yentl*, it would have been a whole different kettle of fish. It could work. *Exterior detail is a contribution on the part of narrative to dialogue*, it reveals the connection between these two elements of fiction. Even as you allow characters to speak, you should be moving the sensibility of the story along. It's one job, connected by many mutually driven tasks. Just like the dialogue above, you keep moving, in more than one direction, all at once.

The way I started that dialogue is different from the way my friend started his all those years ago. I took a detail from the world around me (the movie), added to it (the soup) and let the conversation work around it. I find the argument within the setting there, whereas my friend was struggling to find the setting within the argument. These are our individual quirks, our own strengths. You have to learn to recognize yours, to use them to connect your disparate skills as a writer into one whole act. Where does the story in the theater go from there? I don't know. Why don't you take it and find out? Send it to me when you are finished.

What makes you want to write a story? Perhaps you see an odd chap on the street, limping along, dragging a shopping bag full of oyster shells and you think, *"There's got to be a story there."* Perhaps you remember an old friend, the way he stuck to his guns in the middle of an argument you once had, and think that was something worthy. Perhaps you see patterns in your life—the children at the beach, the birds in your backyard, all of them leaving—and the mood strikes you. Maybe you throw a line down and see where it wants to go. It doesn't matter. The trick is to be self-conscious about what works for you. Know your quirks.

UNEXPECTED TURNS

This chapter has been about using dialogue to lead you to stories. This book has focused on crafting the voices of your characters more clearly and effectively. I'm proposing that you let your characters, or more specifically their dialogues, lead you to new places.

Remember the false triangle from chapter four? There we differentiated between the primary audience and the secondary audience. It was Aristotle who first proposed that all dramatic dialogue has two audiences, hence each line of dialogue, each moment of dramatic exchange has two entirely different meanings. This is an idea that's pretty intuitive for any writer. The primary audience is the person being spoken to, the person to whom the words are directed. The secondary audience is the actual audience (in a theater) or the reader. The writer, according to Aristotle, is in a kind of conversation with both audiences. Remember that the false triangle failed as a model because the meaning was directed primarily at the reader rather than the other characters. That's an understandable mistake. The relationship between the writer and the secondary audience is probably the most easily understood. We write because we read. Within a story, things happen, words are spoken, for the benefit of the reader. When done well, these mechanisms blend into the story seamlessly.

I'm not going to blather on and on about Aristotle. You should be reading that stuff anyway. Get busy. What I'm going to propose is a third audience. Nobody's going to be citing Chiarella in two thousand years (I am clearly more of a Roman than a Greek, by habit and gene), but I am suggesting that you, the writer, become a sort of third audience to dialogue. Listen to your characters. Listen to your world. Within the process of writing, become an audience to your characters. Most people don't tune in as easily to the idea of a writer in conversation with his characters, but anyone who has written knows the writer assumes the persona of his characters when they speak; he speaks *through* his characters to other characters. Now I'm asking you to listen to them. Let them ramble. Let them take you to unexpected places.

The idea is to start with your character's words. Don't start with a conceit. Start with a word. Don't start in a place. Start with a word. Don't start with a conflict. A word! Say the word. Hear the word. Now you are audience to yourself.

Do it long enough, do it hard enough, record enough of what you think and hear and see and you'll start to be able to form a context and circumstance that is surprising, even to you, the one who thinks she knows herself so well. The idea is that the story will take you places. The characters will tell you things. Sometimes you can sit back and listen to your characters. Don't expect much. They may just tell you where the FoodMax is. Just have faith in them. But they may show you things you've only half-known all your life.

EXERCISES

1. Reframe a conversation. Choose one of your existing dialogues. Strip it to a bare-boned exchange, eliminating the original scene. Now ask someone to create a list of five concrete details from the world. Tell him to vary the list. He might hit all the senses or choose a detail from five separate locales. Have him give you his list on an index card. Tape the index card to your computer monitor, or carry it with you, but in any case, read it several times. Then begin rewriting the original dialogue by pulling these details in. You may have to reshape the location, the setting and the circumstance, but work within your original dialogue as much as possible at the start. As you proceed, allow the dialogue to react to these new elements. Characters might pause in new spots, be more willing to reveal what they are after or be more circumspect, depending on how they react. Let the details into the dialogue. Allow them to lead it to new places.

If you don't have anyone to help you list these details, you might create a list of your own, but make it random. Scour your spiral notebooks. Don't decide you are going to take the scene that takes place in a truck stop and move it to an office building by simply listing five details from the lobby of your nearest skyscraper. Challenge yourself. Choose all kinds of details, from all sorts of places.

Feel free to choose one of the lists below as a starting point too, but try to use each as a group, and avoid choosing five items merely because they are easily connected.

> a bowl of beans
> dishwater
> a paper cut
> cows lowing
> chewing carrots

an old dog
a siren
a blacklight poster
the interstate
McDonald's

an armadillo
blasting caps
a weathered porch
clean underwear
an island

two kites
too much salt
boot prints
tuna salad
a phone ringing

2. Take one or several lines of overheard dialogue and, changing the context and speaker, start a story there. Suppose you heard someone say, "No, no. One shelf up," at the supermarket today. Start there. Open the story with those words—"One shelf up"—and from there, start adding details. A name. A new setting. Think of each sentence as part of the process of focusing your vision. At the end of the first paragraph, if you don't see a scene, start again. Same opening line, different speaker, new setting. Try this four times. Read each one. Examine what has happened within the process of starting four times. Which is most successful? Least? Which is furthest from the dialogue trigger? This exercise can often cue you in on new ways to start longer pieces.

EIGHT

NUTS AND BOLTS

In the introduction to this book, I said there are no hard-and-fast rules when it comes to writing dialogue. That just isn't so, as there are a few particular elements about writing dialogue that are governed by rules, such as punctuation; and other things, for example, your use of adverbs and present participles, are elements for which you should create your own individual hard-and-fast rules.

Where do you go with your questions, especially the ones that may seem silly, about dialogue form and format? In this chapter, you'll find answers to some questions you have asked, and others for questions you never knew had been posed. Some of this is advice. There are a few rules. It's meant to help you set up a few rules of your own, to help you pick apart a few misconceptions, while providing some answers for the sorts of specific questions a writer comes up with when writing dialogue.

ON DIALOGUE TAGS

There are several ways to say "she said." She barked, bellowed, shouted, screamed, whined, worried, wailed and waffled. She moaned, whispered and whimpered. She protested. She cackled, cooed and coaxed. She yelled, stammered, stuttered, chortled, coughed, blared, bleated, trumpeted, sneezed, sniffed, hissed, hacked, hooted, harped, haggled, panted, begged, pleaded and pondered. She posited, questioned, spat, sang, trilled, snickered, expounded, uttered, demanded, gasped, groaned, jeered, jested, jabbered and joked. She pronounced, declared, queried, spewed and spumed.

While she may have done all that, the truth is, she *said* it.

New writers tend to lose faith in the word "said." They think they overuse it. My first piece of advice here is to not worry about it. Use "said" in your dialogue tags and nothing else. Concentrate on the words your characters say and the way they say them. Your first obligation should be to their words. Get the words right first.

Still, if you're worried about using "said" too much, that's understandable. It's a small word, and in the course of a long dialogue, it might be used dozens of times. From the very start of our lives as writers, we are trained not to repeat. I used to have a teacher who razored out repeated words on our papers—focusing on unnecessary words such as "very" and "was" and "really"—so that we were left with actual holes in the graded paper. He would hold each paper up in front of the class and the sunlight would leak through it onto the linoleum. "Repeating is lazy," he said. "The mark of a writer who doesn't care."

Admittedly, there is some problem to using the word "said" over and over. Editing yourself as you work, watching for repetition, varying your word choice—these are fine techniques for strengthening your prose, fiction and nonfiction alike. The word "said" repeated often enough becomes, finally, a beat in the pulse of the language. In particularly short, rapid-fire dialogue, the pulse of this word can become overwhelming. The dialogue is flattened out by the straight repetition of the word.

So in a dialogue that's flat, you're in a real double bind. In that sense, overuse of the word "said" is probably a red flag going up that problems exist elsewhere. Look at the dialogue below.

> "Hi," she said.
> "Hello," he said.
> "Did you have a good day?" she said.
> "I sure did," he said.
> "Good," she said.

It stinks. And the use of "said" is only part of the reason why. In other spots in the book, I've discussed insinuating tension into dialogue. Here most of the dialogue tags are unnecessary, but no amount of engineering can make this dialogue work. Remove all the "said's" from the dialogue tags and it gets no better. It's just tensionless jabber.

The problem, as with most lousy dialogue, exists in the words spoken by the character and in the level of tension between the characters. So remember your first obligation: the character's words.

What about a dialogue that's full of tension? What if the words are coming out right and you want to find a way to ease yourself out of repeating the "said's"? Read the dialogue below out loud. It takes place as a character arrives home after spending the last of his Christmas money on a boa constrictor. He arrives after having been in a fairly serious car accident, and his concern is that his snake, hidden from his wife in a large box, has been injured.

> "You're red," Jeanine said.
> "A snake. I bought a snake," I said.
> "You bought a snake?" she said. "You bought a snake."
> "From Andy . . . ," I said. "I bought the snake from Andy."
> "Oh my God!" Jeanine said. "It's in the box! You brought a snake in here!"
> "No, no," I said.
> "It's in the box," she said. "I know it."
> "Wait, wait. Just a second," I said.
> "Get it out!" she said.
> "Don't," I said.
> "You can't do this," she said. "Not in my house."

There are two points to notice here. The use of said is *not* overwhelming. The dialogue moves forward because of the tension and is not fundamentally interrupted by the use of "said." The tension between these characters drives the scene forward. The second thing to notice is that all of the "said's" do not appear at the end of each line of dialogue. The use and placement of dialogue tags is varied. For instance, many of the dialogue tags are "buried" in the middle of lines. ("It's in the box," she said. "I know it.") *Dialogue tags can and should be buried in the middle of the lines of an individual character.*

BURYING DIALOGUE TAGS

This is very simple really. You take a line of dialogue and find a moment of natural pause. Moments of pause include natural pauses as reflected by punctuation. Look for commas and periods, for moments when the character stutters or gropes for words, or for a moment when the two characters are interrupted. At that point, insert a tag. The key is to make the pause created by the placement of the dialogue tags suit the movement and direction of the character's words.

Here's a single piece of dialogue spoken by one character. Look for spots to bury a dialogue tag.

> "Ellie, I'm frustrated. I've been living a double life for years. My life has been a series of bad decisions, and now I'm trying to change."

Picking a point to bury a dialogue tag here is fairly easy. Looking at the sentence again, I'll place markers at potential spots for the tag.

> "Ellie, (1) I'm frustrated. (2) I've been living a double life for years. My life has been a series of bad decisions, (3) and now I'm trying to change."

Placing a tag at 1 ("Ellie," she said . . .) has the effect of pausing the reader before a fairly long expression or sentiment. What follows, follows quickly and in one fell swoop. Placing the tag at 2 ("Ellie, I'm frustrated," she said.) emphasizes the first statement and frames the rest of what follows. Here the dialogue tag balances and focuses the sentiment that follows, on the force of the first declarative statement. Placing the tag at the third spot creates quite a different effect ("My life has been a series of bad decisions," she said, "and now I'm trying to change."), emphasizing the turn the speaker herself is indicating. The placement of the tag "said" therefore alters the meaning of the line.

If we return to the notion of "said" and how much is too much, it should be noted that burying dialogue tags is a way to make "said's" less obtrusive and repetitious. When done right, a dialogue does not need to rely upon changing "said" to "responded" or "screamed" or "whispered." These variations call attention to themselves, and to the writer, rather than the scene. Using "said" keeps the reader focused on the character's words rather than the writer's cleverness. My advice is to stick to "said" until you get the tone and movement right.

VARIATION: ALTERNATIVES TO "SHE SAID" OR "HE SAID"

In my first stories, I made a rule for myself: I would only use the word "said" once within a given dialogue. I figured that in a longish short story, of, say, 25 pages, there might be five to seven sizable dialogues. That meant I only had to "repeat" the word "said" five or six times. Like all rules about writing, it was something to learn from and then, when the time was right, abandon.

Following my rule meant that I would have to vary the words I used in dialogue tags. Consider this snake-in-the-box dialogue again, this time as an example of the rule I set up. I use the word "said" in the first dialogue tag. Look for the moments where it works when I back away from the "said's." You'll notice too that now I've started to apply some of my own watchwords in other ways, burying dialogue tags and insinuating action into the dialogue, revealing the physical scene where possible. These techniques, in variation, allowed the pattern of my dialogues to shift and grow.

"You're red," Jeanine said when I walked in the apartment, my arms slung around the huge box marked FRAGILE: EGGS.

"A snake," I huffed. "I bought a snake." The huge box shifted in my arms.

"You bought a snake?" she sneered, turning a page in her magazine. "You bought a snake." Now she was saying it just to hear herself.

"From Andy . . . ," I paused. The bottom of the box was wet. My new snake. "I bought the snake from Andy."

"Oh my God!" Jeanine shouted. "It's in the box! You brought a snake in here!" She was screaming now, rising from the couch, arming herself by rolling the magazine.

I turned from her. "No, no."

"It's in the box," she snarled. "I know it." She swiped with the magazine, herding me out toward the sunshine.

"Wait, wait," I cringed. The snake slid forward in the box. "Just a second," I shouted.

"Get it out!" she screamed.

The bottom of the box sagged, and I grabbed for it. "Don't hit me!" I shouted. "Don't!"

"You can't do this," she hissed. "Not in my house."

At that point, the box tore and the snake, soaked in its own urine and blood, thumped onto Jeanine's white carpet like a huge, fleshy pipe. I saw right away it was dead.

"My God," she moaned, "a snake. You really did bring in a snake."

Frankly, I remember this rule with fondness, mostly because it taught me variation and pace. As I went on writing a scene, I found myself waiting as long as possible before I used the word "said" as I only allowed myself the one instance. I often held onto it until I could not see another way. Holding off on using "said" lent a certain tension between me and the words that went on the page. I grew to not like simply changing "said" to a descriptive tag, such as "murmured" or "chortled." I started to find ways to make the words themselves contain the charge and energy I was looking for.

But I have long since abandoned this rule, and I just as quickly leave it behind when it comes to teaching. In the above dialogue, the rule was handcuffing me by the middle of the passage. The effect was to bounce the reader between the huffs and the snarls, rather than between the two people. Had I been able to use a few more "said's," I could have leaned on the words a bit more, pushed my sense of their voices more. *If the words of the characters are charged and chosen, they don't need the help of a descriptive dialogue tag.*

What follows is that same dialogue written without any descriptive dialogue tags. Notice that I wasn't always forced to use "said," that the rhythm of the conversation and the use of gesture does the work in many cases.

"You're red," Jeanine said when I walked in the apartment, my arms slung around the huge box marked FRAGILE: EGGS.

"A snake," I said, "I bought a snake." The huge box shifted in my arms.

"You bought a snake?" She sneered a bit, then turned a page in her magazine. "You bought a snake." Now she was saying it just to hear herself.

"From Andy . . . ," The bottom of the box was wet. My new snake. "I bought the snake from Andy."

"Oh my God! It's in the box! You brought a snake in here!" She was screaming now, rising from the couch, arming herself by rolling the magazine.

I turned from her. "No, no."

"It's in the box," she declared. "I know it." She swiped with the magazine, herding me out toward the sunshine.

"Wait, wait." The snake slid forward in the box. "Just a second."

"Get it out!"

The bottom of the box sagged, and I grabbed for it. "Don't hit me!" I said. "Don't!"

She hissed at me. "You can't do this. Not in my house."

At that point, the box tore and the snake, soaked in its own urine and blood, thumped onto Jeanine's white carpet like a huge, fleshy pipe. I saw right away it was dead.

"My God," she said, "a snake. You really did bring in a snake."

In this version of the dialogue, action replaces a dialogue tag ("I turned from her. 'No, no.'"), a descriptive tag is turned into an active verb ("she hissed" is transformed into "She hissed at me."), and a straight dialogue tag is replaced by a descriptive tag for emphasis ("declared" is used to capture the tone of pronouncement and surety). Also we see points where it is obvious who is speaking even when we see no dialogue tag at all ("Get it out!"). These are all variations, designed to keep the reader listening to the dialogue and watching the present action. I've replaced descriptive tags because I felt they were tonally disruptive and distancing.

When to Use Descriptive Tags

Okay, now I've talked about when not to use descriptive tags. But they can't be ignored entirely, right? So when do you use them? As you know, I'll say rarely. But when you do use them, be aware that they affect tone. My advice is to pick them because you can hear some hint of the tone you are shooting for in the tag itself, before the words are attached. Look at the list I gave you at the beginning of this section. I'll reproduce it here in columns. Pick any two words.

barked	bellowed	shouted	screamed
whined	worried	wailed	waffled
moaned	whispered	whimpered	protested
cackled	cooed	coaxed	yelled
stammered	stuttered	chortled	coughed

blared	bleated	trumpeted	sneezed
sniffed	hissed	hacked	hooted
harped	haggled	panted	begged
pleaded	pondered	posited	questioned
spat	sang	trilled	snickered
expounded	uttered	demanded	gasped
groaned	jeered	jested	jabbered
joked	pronounced	declared	queried
spewed	spumed		

Do you know anyone who speaks that way? Say you chose "hacked" and "trumpeted." Do you know anyone who hacks when she speaks? What does the word suggest to you? For me, the word is evocative of a smoker, someone older, someone prone to barking out orders. The word "hacked" cuts against the air; it's a harsh sound. I let the tag lead me to character. I can't see a fourteen-year-old hacking out words, unless he were coughing. He might be really sick, or trying his first cigarette even. Write a line of dialogue in which you use "hacked" as the descriptive tag.

"Yes," she hacked, "I would like some more sherry."

Not bad. Now this is my line, not yours, but I can tell you that I'm thinking about that older person I described above. I see her holding out a glass, suppressing her chronic smoker's cough. When I read the line, I think the tone of her words doesn't match the tone of the tag. I'll make it more of a bark, a command.

"Yes," she hacked, "more sherry."

When you start playing with descriptive tags, they can really lead you places. My mind is in the room with that woman now. I can begin to see the edges of things, the fine rugs, the polished woodwork, the heavy cut-glass ashtrays. I have never been here before either. I am starting to draw this on the basis of what I feel in the character, which came out of the choice of "hacked" and all that it suggested to me.

What if I changed the tag to my other choice, "trumpeted"?

"Yes," she trumpeted, "I would like some more sherry."

I just lost my original speaker, the old woman with the smoker's cough. Now I'm hearing a different voice. Who trumpets? A person prone to enthusiasm, to overstatement. It calls up celebration to me, and for this person, who's obviously been asked if she'd like another drink, trumpeting something might be a declaration of who she is. I see her as loud now, holding little back, as someone who calls attention to herself easily and without pause. To make the tone of the words suit the tag, I would make a few changes.

"Why, yes," she trumpeted, "I'd love some more sherry!"

Now I see a party, or a gathering, perhaps in the same place, but in an entirely different circumstance. The descriptive tag led me there. The list of tags I used was fun to create, and it's fun to read too. There's a sort of writer who treasures the ability to play with and manipulate language over all else. These sorts of tags are one tool of a peculiar and powerful wit, but they can be used by all writers to lead them to new characters, or toward better understanding of the characters who already exist.

NO DIALOGUE TAGS

Some people don't want to use any dialogue tags. They seem to think they get in the way. This can work. Here's a dialogue between two people sitting in the rain.

> "Just wait until this is over."
> "That could be hours."
> "Hours."
> "Hours."
> "But you said we would go get the money."
> "I know I did. We will. We have to wait out the rain."
> "Well that's my concern. I need that money."
> "I'm aware of that. But that's why we wait."

The first guy wants to wait. He urges the other guy to wait out the rain. The other guy wants to go for the money. The dialogue has a conflict, something that sets the two of them against one another in the things they need and want. Easily understandable without dialogue tags, right?

If you were paying careful attention, you were following from one character to the other and you'll see that the first guy ("Just wait until this is over.") actually starts speaking where the second one ought to so that by the end, the second guy is actually the one saying to wait. The dialogue slogs along from there. We become aware of the boundaries for the argument, but it's hard to know which voice is which, and more disturbingly, it ends up being less important which one is which. Chart it with names and you'll see where the mix-up occurs.

Ethan: Just wait until this is over.
Red: That could be hours.
Ethan: Hours.
Red: Hours.
Ethan: But you said we would go get the money.
Red: I know I did. We will. We have to wait out the rain.
Ethan: Well that's my concern. I need that money.
Red: I'm aware of that. But that's why we wait.

Still, most readers would barrel though that. There's something to be learned from the pace of that dialogue. But it's important to note that the alternation was not enough to keep the characters separate for us. Use untagged dialogue advisedly, but surely try it. It works particularly well when two people are caught in a long, fast-moving dialogue, where the needs of the characters define them as well as any dialogue tag could. Stephen Crane's "The Open Boat" features four men trapped in a lifeboat, caught in the open sea. The story moves for pages without any dialogue tags, and the initial effect is that the reader is never sure exactly who is speaking in any one line. The effect is purposeful though, as the reader begins to separate the men gradually and subtly. For a large portion of the story, they are trapped within sight of land but are unable to make a run for shore against the surf. Read the passage below. Watch to see where you can pick up on who is speaking.

"There's a man on shore!"
"Where?"
"There? See 'im? See 'im?"
"Yes, sure! He's walking along."
"Now he's stopped. Look! He's facing us!"
"He's waving at us!"
"So he is! By thunder!"
"Ah, now, we're all right! There'll be a boat out here for us in half an hour."

It is impossible to say who is speaking when, and in what order. But here the lack of dialogue tags suits the effect of the story, which is to blend the four voices into one swirling mass of hope and uncertainty. The technique reflects the circumstance that it depicts. I'm not saying there is no other use for this sort of dialogue. There are plenty around, and plenty yet to be invented. But read for and understand the effect of the technique you choose. Like the other uses of dialogue tags mentioned here, use it wisely, in variation with the others. The key is to find a rhythm that suits you.

THE EXCLAMATION POINT

I had a friend, a sweet-hearted writer named Gabby Hyman, who taught me a good watchword on the exclamation point. He claimed his teacher taught him this, and that may be so, but by the time I got it, this was old advice. He said he only used exclamation points when he wanted the effect of what he was saying to be "boing!" You know "boing," the old cartoon sound of a spring uncoiling.

> "Why yes!" Boing!
> "I love gravy!" Boing!
> "Take that ball away!" Boing!

I love the general spirit of this rule. The idea of attaching a sound to a piece of punctuation is marvelous. Periods could be thumps, question marks could sound like doorbells. There are times when that sound, that effect of "boing," is not all that bad. It might be something you want. But clearly my friend meant that as a warning not to use too many exclamation points. I have found that there are times when whispering "boing!" to yourself when you type an exclamation point might save you some trouble.

The trouble you get into with exclamation points is pretty easy to understand. Young writers tend to think of them as points of emphasis. For them an exclamation point reads, "I really mean it!" Children love them. Here's my son's first letter to me.

> I am! I am mad!

Wow! Boing! The idea of saying "boing" as a writer is to remind yourself that the writer has authority, the reader knows the author means it and the exclamation point is not usually necessary.

Still, I've come to use exclamation points more as I get older. To me they represent earnestness rather than comic overstatement, though they surely can be used for either. And more. Understand the effect. You might start with the "boing rule," which will have the effect of making you use fewer exclamation points. From there, you might adopt another sound. There are many writers, from Mark Leyner to Nicholson Baker, for whom the exclamation point is a sharp-edged tool. I see it used well all the time. But you have to think, *What effect does the exclamation point have?* I've used it all through this book. My suggestion is to create your own sound effect to whisper to yourself whenever you use the exclamation point. That will help you produce music, through discipline.

ON ADVERBS
Recently I was reading a draft of a story that included this line.

"I love my home," she said quaintly. "I always have."

I paused at the moment I read the word "quaintly" and felt the urge to say exactly what she said aloud. How does one say that quaintly? Try it. Say it right now. But say it quaintly. Where does the emphasis fall?

"I *love* my home."
"I love my *home*."
"I love *my* home."

Perhaps you could add a southern accent to it? Or you could say it slowly and evenly so it sounded measured and practiced. No, even as you speak, the first seems too cliché, the second too calculating. Perhaps you could hold your hands in your lap as you say it. That would be quaint, in a certain sense.

The truth is, it's hard to say something quaintly. Impossible really. The trouble isn't the sense of the word "quaint"; it's using the word as an adverb. They tend to be trouble.

Should I tell you never to use adverbs? Rules like that irk me, but for now, okay: Never use adverbs, at least never use them within dialogue tags. It seems pretty harsh to say that, but there are good reasons. Adverbs tempt the reader to think more about *the way* something is said than about *what* is actually said. Remember that a verb describes an action already. An adverb merely qualifies an action. Using, more particularly, overusing, adverbs shifts the reader's focus from the words themselves to the speaker's accent, lilt and pace in speaking them. Speaking is an act of will. It doesn't need much in the way of qualification.

Use actions and reactions to frame a dialogue. Reactions are good, part of the give-and-take of the whole. Yes, you want the words to cause reaction, but you want the reaction to be something tangible, such as flinching, not something loose and limpid, easily ignored, such as flinchingly.

Replace the adverbs in the dialogue below using gestures, shifting adverbs to adjectives, looking to the scene for your reaction.

> "Has Bobbi seen this yet?" she said *dryly*.
> "No, and I'm not going to show it to her until it's written in stone," Wilma said *tersely*.
> "Frankly, I don't think that's smart," Kay said, *grinningly*. "I know what she'll say."
> "We all think she'll be unhappy," Wilma responded *knowingly*.

An exaggeration, admittedly. But look at the italicized adverbs. Each is guilty of an effect that takes away from dialogue. The first—"dryly"—might be the most effective, but it's exactly the sort of thing that can be handled with a solid treatment of character, a declarative to set the pace ("Her tone was dry and detached, as usual"). *Adverbs tend to take the place of description, unnecessarily so.* The second—"tersely"—simply restated the tone and pace of what was said. The words "No, and I'm not going to show it to her until it's written in stone" are terse already. This is another problem with adverbs. *When used in strong dialogue, adverbs can become redundant.* The fourth adverb—"knowingly"—is guilty of much the same thing as the second, although this time it merely echoes the sentiment of the speaker rather than the pace or rhythm of what's being said. She's saying she knows, and she's saying it knowingly. The reader's response ought to be "Duh!" The third adverb—"grinningly"—is mawkish and contrived. It is an attempt to keep from saying "with a grin," which might sound too chipper, or "grinning," which seems comic. But the word "grinningly," which may not even be a word so far as I know, is such an ugly creation and pushes the reader to think about the process of grinning rather than about the words being spoken. In addition, note that the speaker also used an adverb—"frankly"—and the adverb in the dialogue tag appears too close on the heels of that. Read the entire line aloud, tag and all, and you'll start to see the effect. Remember I am not saying that people don't use adverbs when they speak. I am saying not to use them when you, as a writer, describe the way in which they speak. Finally, unless used advisedly, *adverbs can make dialogue sound contrived.*

PRESENT PARTICIPLES

"Oh, the participle," he said, *gently scratching his armpit.* "It can be an onerous business."

It's okay to refine your action by using a participle. You may be walking, thinking through your day. Or thinking through your day, scratching that sore on your elbow and humming a melancholy tune, you might pause. You may say something to the person next to you at the White Castle, while wiping the mustard from you chin. That's certainly been done. There's nothing wrong with it.

> "There," I said, wiping my napkin across my chin, "we've reached the limit."

Adding participles doesn't hurt, when you do it wisely. One is fine. Two can work, but a back-and-forth of participles does nothing but diffuse the dialogue.

> "There," I said, wiping my napkin across my chin, "we've reached the limit."
> "What are you talking about?" she said, tapping the edge of the table.
> "I'm sick of this," I said, glancing out the window.
> Reaching for the ketchup, she snorted. "You're so afraid of conflict," she said, taking a bite.
> "You're right," I said, pulling closer to the table. I focused on her forehead, zeroing in on the wrinkles there. "I'm afraid. I'm afraid and I'm tired." I glanced up, checking the time subtly.

That doesn't work. It's not a bad dialogue really. The story is there, both before and after this scene. It sounds like two people speaking.

143

But you have to fight the gesture to get at the words they speak. As much as I've harped about adding gesture, incorporating scene, there is a limit. Why focus on participles? Participles are the first means most writers rely on for attaching action to the words being spoken.

PUNCTUATION

People always want to know about punctuating dialogue. It is truly very simple. First remember that **the punctuation always goes inside the quote**. That's the first mistake many people make. This example is correct.

"It's as simple as the smile on your face," he said.

This is incorrect.

"It's a complicated issue", he answered.

Beyond that, understand that **the dialogue tag frames the sentence in which it appears**.

"It's as hard as a rock," he said.

The period appears after the dialogue tag. The following would be incorrect.

"It's like a candle in the wind." he said.

Other forms of terminal punctuation appear inside the quotes. Exclamation points and question marks come to mind. The dialogue tag still acts as a part of a longer sentence; it is *not* capitalized.

"I like my pudding!" she exclaimed.
"You want me to turn it over?" she said.

Terminal punctuation is never followed by a comma. The following would be incorrect.

"Tell it to the Marines!," she blurted.
"Don't you want me to speak French for you?," she said.

Keep in mind that the dialogue tag frames the longer sentence in which it appears. **When placed in the center of a long line of dialogue, the tag acts as a pause, surrounded on either side by quotes**.

"Red, I'm worried about your fingers," he said, "and the damage we've done to them by placing you in the middle of this insane experiment!"

Notice that the dialogue tag is punctuated by commas on either side because it appears in the middle of a long, complete sentence. The following would be incorrect, since both halves of the dialogue are complete sentences.

"Don't tell me those things are water rats," she said nervously, "They're dock rats and they're not afraid of anything."
"I'm quite certain of it," he added, "In fact, if you'll just hand me a twenty dollar bill, I'll prove it to you."

To punctuate these correctly, you would simply change the comma at the end of the dialogue tag to a period and treat the next sentence as an individual unit.

"I don't like ale," he said. "I like beer. As far as I'm concerned, there's no such thing as ale."

If two people speak, without pause, or without a dialogue tag between them, it is customary to begin a new paragraph. The following would be correct.

"I've never stolen anything in my life."
"Think twice before you lie."

While it would not be incorrect per se to set them back to back, it might be confounding.

"I've never stolen anything in my life." "Think twice before you lie."

This back-to-back approach is confusing, and it can get even more so when the writer, with the intention of clarifying, places a dialogue tag in the middle.

"I've never stolen anything in my life," he said. "I believe it too. You're as straight as they come."

Whenever someone new speaks up, indicate the exchange by beginning a new paragraph.

"I've never stolen anything in my life," he said, eyeballing the jewelry display.

"Don't think of it as stealing. Think of it as larceny. It suits you better."

If a character speaks for an extended period and you want to begin a new paragraph, it is not necessary to close the quotes at the end of the first paragraph. This sample is correct.

"Interrogations happen when you do something wrong," the agent said. "Retraining is all about doing it right. Look, we accept that the mind follows the body. Right? The mind follows the body! Poppycock. Bullshit. Rot and drivel. The mind *is* the body! Interrogations? Doomed to fail. You shock someone, I mean really shock him—cattle prod, 2.5 liter spray bottle of ionized water, metal chair, puddle of urine—the whole nine yards—and all you do is issue an invitation to the mind.

"You ask so little! Yet threaten with all your heart, and still the mind does not follow. The mind does not follow. Get me? State of mind. Know the expression? Sure, you do. State of being. State of mind. Coincidence? Hell, no! They're the same thing. You see? The mind *is* being."

One can always invent circumstances in which punctuating dialogue is more tricky than this. Some writers don't punctuate their dialogue and use only dialogue tags to do the work of indicating the exchange. The effect here is mostly aesthetic.

You can't kill me, she said. You just can't.

Some writers think it is somehow more elemental to strip away the punctuation. I suppose it is a matter of taste. Not using punctuation affects the pace of the writing and, in some cases, might blur the lines between speakers. But I can't see much to recommend it. Do it if you want, but do it consistently. My sense is that if you concern yourself with the act of typing in order to produce an effect in your fiction, you are creating a kind of flea circus with your characters and little more. Writing should be about writing, not typing. Learn the rules of punctuation, or set up some new rules, but in either case, live with them, then get on with the act of writing.

ITALICS AND FONTS

I can still remember the days, not all that long ago, when I was interested in italics. They seemed an elaborate and expensive device. The same with fonts. Less than twenty years ago, the word "font" was just another word for "fountain," and Times Roman would have been taken to be a reference to an Italian edition of *The New York Times.*

I'm always happy when time passes and change limps through. I compose on a computer now, with seventy-four fonts a mere double-click away. Even italics just take a short mouse roll. I have no regrets. It's much better this way. But the truth is, I see so many young writers attempting to solve problems by manipulating the presentation on the page (students routinely manipulate font to increase page length, center justification is employed to make things look "neat," etc.) that I feel compelled to warn against it.

I like italics. As I said, they used to be a rare commodity, a tool of the published or the rich. I once had access to an IBM Selectric with a changeable typeface. I remember that in one weekend, I retyped all my poems that needed italics and then I wrote poems entirely in italics, then I alternated words, until changing the type wheel became so routine I tired of it and was left with my lousy poems to rewrite, which I began to do, using italics less and less. I came to a point where changing the type wheel was more trouble than it was worth. I happily gave the typewriter back.

When word processing programs came on the scene, italics were thrown open as a possibility to everyone, and that is the way it should be. There are uses for italics in dialogue. I like the standard use best. *Emphasis. Accent.* When you want the speaker to really lean into a word, italics are a good way of indicating emphasis. You can put a whole sentence in italics from time to time, but it ought to be short, the kind that can be accented naturally, without some elaborate read-back.

These are okay in my book.

> "I'm talking about life on another *planet*, Simpson," he said.
> "*Cut it out!*" she said.

These are not okay in my book.

> "*I am concerned* with these *discrepancies*, Troy," he barked.
> "There's *trouble* ahead." (Too elaborate.)

"I'm *feeling* a *pain* in my *chest*," Gerry said. "It's like someone *punched* me." (Unnecessarily replaces natural points of accent.)

Many times writers will use italics to indicate the voice of another speaker, a voice from the past, a voice of the consciousness, a voice unheard by all except the protagonist, or even by the reader alone. This seems a reasonable variation to me, again prone to overuse. Use it with caution, as any typographic trick—including boldface and underlining—can become mawkish and confining when used simply for effect. If emphasis is what you are shooting for, a more active verb is almost always the best bet.

No trick is more tiresome than the font change, however. There are writers who use different fonts to indicate the voices of different speakers. Let me try to dissuade you from this bit of typographic pyrotechnics. It is tedious.

It's a product of self-publishing and 'zine culture. I love 'zines. I have created my own. But putting together your own magazine, "laying out" your story in a graphic-heavy environment, is an act more akin to painting than to writing. It's visual. It's valuable, just unrelated to the act of writing. Nothing against 'zines here. They rock.

Still, I don't care what anyone says, font changes are just exemplars of people with too much time on their hands and not enough interest in, or knowledge of, what they are attempting when they start to write.

Don't do them.

EXERCISES

1. Start a dialogue between two people purposefully using no dialogue tags whatsoever. Write two full pages. If you are stuck for an idea, use one of the following.

- an argument over a bag of money
- a minor revelation on a ski lift
- a conversation between a hitchhiker and the driver who picks him up

Now prepare yourself to rewrite the dialogue three times.

A. On the first pass, work to find ways other than dialogue tags to indicate who the speaker of a given line is. Use gestures, actions and elements of scene to help direct the reader. Be precise in the exchange. There's no need to indicate every exchange with a gesture though. At the end of this pass, go back and eliminate any clumsy gestures or awkward movements.

B. On second pass, allow yourself to fill in with a limited number of dialogue tags. Say, five over the course of two pages. Use them only where they are needed most. Use no two dialogue tags the same way. That is to say, use one straight dialogue tag at the end of a line, use one descriptive dialogue tag, use one tag with adverb, bury one in the middle of a line, start one line with the tag if you can. Don't clump these variations together either. Use judgment.

C. Now, on the final pass, keeping everything in place, add straight dialogue tags ("he said," "she said" and "[name] said"). Add them for the sake of clarity. Try to leave several lines unadorned by tags. If that's not possible, march on and fill them all in. You should have enough variation built in already to avoid trouble.

Try to remember this sequence; it's helpful in creating dialogue that is varied and rhythmic. In any case, start with the words, stay with the words and let the dialogue tags serve you and the reader only in understanding the dialogue better.

2. Start a dialogue with a single line and work from there. Give the line a standard tag, for instance, "he said." Now add an adverb to that tag. If you need a situation, use one of these.

- Three people in a white-water raft, moving toward a dangerous set of rapids
- Two sisters who have discovered their father was embezzling money from his law firm
- A father and a son at the kitchen table about the sports page; the father is hiding something

Here's the twist: Add the first adverb and write from there. Write one page. Now go back and start again from the first line, changing only the adverb. In what ways does this small detail lead you to new places? Is it possible to recreate the dialogue even with this change in tone? If so, try for a stronger adverb, something quite the opposite of the first. If you can still work pretty much within the confines of your first dialogue, take a long hard look at the dialogue itself. In what ways can you charge the language? How can you vary the pace? Where can you pick up on new tensions? Try this two or three times. Then, using the strongest dialogue you create, remove the adverb and show the result to someone. Does he have any problem picking up on the tone and tension of the piece? Odds are, if he does, you were relying too much on the adverb and not enough on the words of the characters themselves.

AFTERWORD

There it is. You've gotten my best advice on writing dialogue. Now let me give you my advice from the introduction again. Work.

It's my hope that this book didn't merely give you a sense of what's wrong with bad dialogue, but that it helped you to see what's right in yours. After you teach creative writing long enough, you start to recognize the "rules" junkies, those people who want to have a rule for every circumstance. What they quickly learn is that there's no point. For every suggestion I make in this book about what doesn't work, there's probably a living writer who is doing just that and doing it well. For instance, in the introduction I said, "Or one writer's characters sound like fortune cookies . . . ," implying, I think, that there's something wrong with that. I was in New York last month, standing in a bookstore, when the person I was with picked up a book by Mark Leyner, whose work I like very much, and said, "This is great. Everything sounds like an infomercial and everyone talks like a fortune cookie."

"And you like that?" I said.

"Sure," my companion said. "That's my world in a nutshell."

I shrugged. That's the way it is. Good dialogue, like good stories in general, captures part of the larger world and shows it to us. Feel free to work against everything I've told you in this book. But work. That was my advice, way back when I thought dialogue that sounded like fortune cookies was a bad idea. No wait, that was a rule. Work.

APPENDIX

In this book we've looked at excerpts from fiction and film, radio and television, focusing on the role of dialogue in individual scenes. But to fully understand that role, we need to study an entire narrative, beginning to ending. This approach allows us to examine how dialogue works in harmony with other elements of storytelling, such as exposition and description.

The following story, "Bliss," appeared in *Bliss and Other Stories* by Katherine Mansfield, published in 1920. Mansfield was an innovative story writer who, as you'll notice when reading "Bliss," relied much on dialogue. She's worth studying. Though her characters use trendy slang that is now, of course, dated—as are their pretensions and posturings—their voices are still vibrant and particular.

As you read this story, focus on those voices. What makes them work? And try to identify Mansfield's use of techniques that we've discussed in this book. Notice the pace of the dialogue and how it moves the narrative forward; notice how dialogue is used to characterize; notice the use of slang, dialect, idiom; notice how some characters have verbal tics that are so distinct Mansfield doesn't even have to use dialogue tags: We know immediately who is speaking.

BLISS

Although Bertha Young was thirty she still had moments like this when she wanted to run instead of walk, to take dancing steps on and off the pavement, to bowl a hoop, to throw something up in the air and catch it again, or to stand still and laugh at—nothing—at nothing, simply.

What can you do if you are thirty and, turning the corner of your own street, you are overcome, suddenly, by a feeling of bliss—absolute bliss!—as though you'd suddenly swallowed a bright piece of that late afternoon sun and it burned in your bosom, sending out a little shower of sparks into every particle, into every finger and toe . . . ?

Oh, is there no way you can express it without being "drunk and disorderly"? How idiotic civilization is! Why be given a body if you have to keep it shut up in a case like a rare, rare fiddle?

"No, that about the fiddle is not quite what I mean," she thought, running up the steps and feeling in her bag for the key—she'd forgotten it, as usual—and rattling the letter-box. "It's not what I mean, because—Thank you, Mary"—she went into the hall. "Is nurse back?"

"Yes, M'm."

"And has the fruit come?"

"Yes, M'm. Everything's come."

"Bring the fruit up to the dining-room, will you? I'll arrange it before I go upstairs."

It was dusky in the dining-room and quite chilly. But all the same Bertha threw off her coat; she could not bear the tight clasp of it another moment, and the cold air fell on her arms.

But in her bosom there was still that bright glowing place— that shower of little sparks coming from it. It was almost unbearable. She hardly dared to breath for fear of fanning it higher, and yet she breathed deeply, deeply. She hardly dared to look into the cold mirror—but she did look, and it gave her back a woman, radiant, with smiling, trembling lips, with big, dark eyes and an air of listening, waiting for something . . . divine to happen . . . that she knew must happen . . . infallibly.

Mary brought in the fruit on a tray and with it a glass bowl, and a blue dish, very lovely, with a strange sheen on it as though it had been dipped in milk.

"Shall I turn on the light, M'm?"

"No, thank you. I can see quite well."

There were tangerines and apples stained with strawberry pink. Some yellow pears, smooth as silk, some white grapes covered with a silver bloom and a big cluster of purple ones. These last she had bought to tone in with the new living-room carpet. Yes, that did sound rather far-fetched and absurd, but it was really why she had bought them. She had thought in the shop: "I must have some purple ones to bring the carpet up to the table." And it had seemed quite sense at the time.

When she had finished with them and had made two pyramids of these bright round shapes, she stood away from the table to get the effect—and it really was most curious. For the dark table seemed to melt into the dusky light and the glass dish and the blue bowl to float in the air. This, of course, in her present mood, was so incredibly beautiful. . . . She began to laugh.

"No, no. I'm getting hysterical." And she seized her bag and coat and ran upstairs to the nursery.

Nurse sat at a low table giving Little B her supper after her bath. The baby had on a white flannel gown and a blue woollen jacket, and her dark, fine hair was brushed up into a funny little peak. She looked up when she saw her mother and began to jump.

"Now, my lovey, eat it up like a good girl," said Nurse, setting her lips in a way that Bertha knew, and that meant she had come into the nursery at another wrong moment.

"Has she been good, Nanny?"

"She's been a little sweet all the afternoon," whispered Nanny. "We went to the park and I sat down on a chair and took her out of the pram and a big dog came along and put its head on my knee and she clutched its ear, tugged it. Oh, you should have seen her."

Bertha wanted to ask if it wasn't rather dangerous to let her clutch at a strange dog's ear. But she did not dare to. She stood watching them, her hands by her side, like the poor little girl in front of the rich little girl with the doll.

The baby looked up at her again, stared, and then smiled so charmingly that Bertha couldn't help crying:

"Oh, Nanny, do let me finish giving her her supper while you put the bath things away."

"Well, M'm, she oughtn't to be changed hands while she's eating," said Nanny, still whispering. "It unsettles her; it's very likely to upset her."

How absurd it was. Why have a baby if it has to be kept—not in a case like a rare, rare fiddle—but in another woman's arms?

"Oh, I must!" said she.

Very offended, Nanny handed her over.

"Now, don't excite her after her supper. You know you do, M'm. And I have such a time with her after!"

Thank heaven! Nanny went out of the room with the bath towels.

"Now I've got you to myself, my little precious," said Bertha, as the baby leaned against her.

She ate delightfully, holding up her lips for the spoon and then waving her hands. Sometimes she wouldn't let the spoon go; and sometimes, just as Bertha had filled it, she waved it away to the four winds.

When the soup was finished Bertha turned round to the fire.

"You're nice—you're very nice!" said she, kissing her warm baby. "I'm fond of you. I like you."

And, indeed, she loved Little B so much—her neck as she bent forward, her exquisite toes as they shone transparent in the firelight—that all her feeling of bliss came back again, and again she didn't know how to express it—what to do with it.

"You're wanted on the telephone," said Nanny, coming back in triumph and seizing *her* little B.

Down she flew. It was Harry.

"Oh, is that you, Ber? Look here. I'll be late. I'll take a taxi and come along as quickly as I can, but get dinner put back ten minutes—will you? All right?"

"Yes, perfectly. Oh, Harry!"

"Yes?"

What had she to say? She'd nothing to say. She only wanted to get in touch with him for a moment. She couldn't absurdly cry: "Hasn't it been a divine day!"

"What is it?" rapped out the little voice.

"Nothing. *Entendu*," said Bertha, and hung up the receiver, thinking how more than idiotic civilization was.

They had people coming to dinner. The Norman Knights—a very sound couple—he was about to start a theatre, and she was awfully keen on interior decoration, a young man, Eddie Warren, who had just published a little book of poems and whom everybody was asking to dine, and a "find" of Bertha's called Pearl Fulton. What Miss Fulton did, Bertha didn't know.

They had met at the club and Bertha had fallen in love with her, as she always did fall in love with beautiful women who had something strange about them.

The provoking thing was that, though they had been about together and met a number of times and really talked, Bertha couldn't yet make her out. Up to a certain point Miss Fulton was rarely, wonderfully frank, but the certain point was there, and beyond that she would not go.

Was there anything beyond it? Harry said "No." Voted her dullish, and "cold like all blond women, with a touch, perhaps, of anæmia of the brain." But Bertha wouldn't agree with him; not yet, at any rate.

"No, the way she has of sitting with her head a little on one side, and smiling, has something behind it, Harry, and I must find out what that something is."

"Most likely it's a good stomach," answered Harry.

He made a point of catching Bertha's heels with replies of that kind . . . "liver frozen, my dear girl," or "pure flatulence," or "kidney disease," . . . and so on. For some strange reason Bertha liked this, and almost admired it in him very much.

She went into the drawing-room and lighted the fire; then, picking up the cushions, one by one, that Mary had disposed so carefully, she threw them back on to the chairs and the couches. That made all the difference; the room came alive at once. As she was about to throw the last one she surprised herself by suddenly hugging it to her, passionately, passionately. But it did not put out the fire in her bosom. Oh, on the contrary!

The windows of the drawing-room opened on to a balcony overlooking the garden. At the far end, against the wall, there was a tall, slender pear tree in fullest, richest bloom; it stood perfect, as though becalmed against the jade-green sky. Bertha couldn't help feeling, even from this distance, that it had not a single bud or a faded petal. Down below, in the garden beds, the red and yellow tulips, heavy with flowers, seemed to lean upon the dusk. A grey cat, dragging its belly, crept across the lawn, and a black one, its shadow, trailed after. The sight of them, so intent and so quick, gave Bertha a curious shiver.

"What creepy things cats are!" she stammered, and she turned away from the window and began walking up and down. . . .

How strong the jonquils smelled in the warm room. Too strong? Oh, no. And yet, as though overcome, she flung down on a couch and pressed her hands to her eyes.

"I'm too happy—too happy!" she murmured.

And she seemed to see on her eyelids the lovely pear tree with its wide open blossoms as a symbol of her own life.

Really—really—she had everything. She was young. Harry and she were as much in love as ever, and they got on together splendidly and were really good pals. She had an adorable baby. They didn't have to worry about money. They had this absolutely satisfactory house and garden. And friends—modern, thrilling friends, writers and painters and poets or people keen on social questions—just the kind of friends they wanted. And then there were books, and there was music, and she had found a wonderful little dressmaker, and they were going abroad in the summer, and their new cook made the most superb omelettes. . . .

"I'm absurd. Absurd!" She sat up; but she felt quite dizzy, quite drunk. It must have been the spring.

Yes, it was the spring. Now she was so tired she could not drag herself upstairs to dress.

A white dress, a string of jade beads, green shoes and stockings. It wasn't intentional. She had thought of this scheme hours before she stood at the drawing-room window.

Her petals rustled softly into the hall, and she kissed Mrs. Norman Knight, who was taking off the most amusing orange coat with a procession of black monkeys round the hem and up the fronts.

". . . Why! Why! Why is the middle-class so stodgy—so utterly without a sense of humour! My dear, it's only by a fluke that I am here at all—Norman being the protective fluke. For my darling monkeys so upset the train that it rose to a man and simply ate me with its eyes. Didn't laugh—wasn't amused—that I should have loved. No, just stared—and bored me through and through."

"But the cream of it was," said Norman, pressing a large tortoise-shell-rimmed monocle into his eye, "you don't mind me telling this, Face, do you?" (In their home and among their friends they called each other Face and Mug.) "The cream of it was when she, being full fed, turned to the woman beside her and said: 'Haven't you ever seen a monkey before?' "

"Oh, yes!" Mrs. Norman Knight joined in the laughter. "Wasn't that too absolutely creamy?"

And a funnier thing still was that now her coat was off she did look like a very intelligent monkey—who had even made that yellow silk dress out of scraped banana skins. And her amber ear-rings; they were like little dangling nuts.

"This is a sad, sad fall!" said Mug, pausing in front of Little B's perambulator. "When the perambulator comes into the hall—" and he waved the rest of the quotation away.

The bell rang. It was lean, pale Eddie Warren (as usual) in a state of acute distress.

"It *is* the right house, *isn't* it?" he pleaded.

"Oh, I think so—I hope so," said Bertha brightly.

"I have had such a *dreadful* experience with a taxi-man; he was *most* sinister. I couldn't get him to *stop*. The *more* I knocked and called the *faster* he went. And *in* the moonlight this *bizarre* figure with the *flattened* head *crouching* over the *lit-tle* wheel. . . ."

He shuddered, taking off an immense white silk scarf. Bertha noticed that his socks were white, too—most charming.

"But how dreadful!" she cried.

"Yes, it really was," said Eddie, following her into the drawing-room. "I saw myself *driving* through Eternity in a *timeless* taxi."

He knew the Norman Knights. In fact, he was going to write a play for N. K. when the theatre scheme came off.

"Well, Warren, how's the play?" said Norman Knight, dropping his monocle and giving his eye a moment in which to rise to the surface before it was screwed down again.

And Mrs. Norman Knight: "Oh, Mr. Warren, what happy socks!"

"I *am* so glad you like them," said he, staring at his feet. "They seem to have got so *much* whiter since the moon rose."

And he turned his lean sorrowful young face to Bertha. "There *is* a moon, you know."

She wanted to cry: "I am sure there is—often—often!"

He really was a most attractive person. But so was Face, crouched before the fire in her banana skins, and so was Mug, smoking a cigarette and saying as he flicked the ash: "Why doth the bridegroom tarry?"

"There he is, now."

Bang went the front door open and shut. Harry shouted: "Hullo, you people. Down in five minutes." And they heard him swarm up the stairs. Bertha couldn't help smiling; she knew how he loved doing things at high pressure. What, after all, did an extra five minutes matter? But he would pretend to himself that they mattered beyond measure. And then he would make a great point of coming into the drawing-room, extravagantly cool and collected.

Harry had such a zest for life. Oh, how she appreciated it in him. And his passion for fighting—for seeking in everything that came up against him another test of his power and of his courage—that, too, she understood. Even when it made him just occasionally, to other people, who didn't know him well, a little ridiculous perhaps. . . . For there were moments when he rushed into battle where no battle was. . . . She talked and laughed and positively forgot until he had come in (just as she had imagined) that Pearl Fulton had not turned up.

"I wonder if Miss Fulton has forgotten?"

"I expect so," said Harry. "Is she on the 'phone?"

"Ah! There's a taxi, now." And Bertha smiled with that little air of proprietorship that she always assumed while her women finds were new and mysterious. "She lives in taxis."

"She'll run to fat if she does," said Harry coolly, ringing the bell for dinner. "Frightful danger for blond women."

"Harry—don't," warned Bertha, laughing up at him.

Came another tiny moment, while they waited, laughing and talking, just a trifle too much at their ease, a trifle too unaware. And then Miss Fulton, all in silver, with a silver fillet binding her pale blond hair, came in smiling, her head a little on one side.

"Am I late?"

"No, not at all," said Bertha. "Come along." And she took her arm and they moved into the dining-room.

What was there in the touch of that cool arm that could fan—fan—start blazing—blazing—the fire of bliss that Bertha did not know what to do with?

Miss Fulton did not look at her; but then she seldom did look at people directly. Her heavy eyelids lay upon her eyes and the strange half smile came and went upon her lips as though she lived by listening rather than seeing. But Bertha knew, suddenly, as if the longest, most intimate look had passed between them—as if they had said to each other: "You, too?"—that Pearl Fulton, stirring the beautiful red soup in the grey plate, was feeling just what she was feeling.

And the others? Face and Mug, Eddie and Harry, their spoons rising and falling—dabbing their lips with their napkins, crumbling bread, fiddling with the forks and glasses and talking.

"I met her at the Alpha show—the weirdest little person. She'd not only cut off her hair, but she seemed to have taken a dreadfully good snip off her legs and arms and her neck and her poor little nose as well."

"Isn't she very *liée* with Michael Oat?"

"The man who wrote *Love in False Teeth*?"

"He wants to write a play for me. One act. One man. Decides to commit suicide. Gives all the reasons why he should and why he shouldn't. And just as he has made up his mind either to do it or not to do it—curtain. Not half a bad idea."

"What's he going to call it—'Stomach Trouble'?"

"I *think* I've come across the *same* idea in a lit-tle French review, *quite* unknown in England."

No, they didn't share it. They were dears—dears—and she loved having them there, at her table, and giving them delicious food and wine. In fact, she longed to tell them how delightful they were, and what a decorative group they made, how they seemed to set one another off and how they reminded her of a play by Tchekof!

Harry was enjoying his dinner. It was part of his—well, not his nature, exactly, and certainly not his pose—his—something or other—to talk about food and to glory in his "shameless passion for the white flesh of the lobster" and "the green of pistachio ices—green and cold like the eyelids of Egyptian dancers."

When he looked up at her and said: "Bertha, this is a very admirable *soufflé!*" she almost could have wept with child-like pleasure.

Oh, why did she feel so tender towards the whole world tonight? Everything was good—was right. All that happened seemed to fill again her brimming cup of bliss.

And still, in the back of her mind, there was the pear tree. It would be silver now, in the light of poor dear Eddie's moon, silver as Miss Fulton, who sat there turning a tangerine in her slender fingers that were so pale a light seemed to come from them.

What she simply couldn't make out—what was miraculous—was how she should have guessed Miss Fulton's mood so exactly and so instantly. For she never doubted for a moment that she was right, and yet what had she to go on? Less than nothing.

"I believe this does happen very, very rarely between women. Never between men," thought Bertha. "But while I am making the coffee in the drawing-room perhaps she will 'give a sign.' "

What she meant by that she did not know, and what would happen after that she could not imagine.

While she thought like this she saw herself talking and laughing. She had to talk because of her desire to laugh.

"I must laugh or die."

But when she noticed Face's funny little habit of tucking something down the front of her bodice—as if she kept a tiny, secret hoard of nuts there, too—Bertha had to dig her nails into her hands—so as not to laugh too much.

It was over at last. And: "Come and see my new coffee machine," said Bertha.

"We only have a new coffee machine once a fortnight," said Harry. Face took her arm this time; Miss Fulton bent her head and followed after.

The fire had died down in the drawing-room to a red, flickering "nest of baby phœnixes," said Face.

"Don't turn up the light for a moment. It is so lovely." And down she crouched by the fire again. She was always cold . . . "without her little red flannel jacket, of course," thought Bertha.

At that moment Miss Fulton "gave the sign."

"Have you a garden?" said the cool, sleepy voice.

This was so exquisite on her part that all Bertha could do was to obey. She crossed the room, pulled the curtains apart, and opened those long windows.

"There!" she breathed.

And the two women stood side by side looking at the slender, flowering tree. Although it was so still it seemed, like the flame of a candle, to stretch up, to point, to quiver in the bright air, to grow taller and taller as they gazed—almost to touch the rim of the round, silver moon.

How long did they stand there? Both, as it were, caught in that circle of unearthly light, understanding each other perfectly, creatures of another world, and wondering what they were to do in this one with all this blissful treasure that burned in their bosoms and dropped, in silver flowers, from their hair and hands?

For ever—for a moment? And did Miss Fulton murmur: "Yes. Just *that*." Or did Bertha dream it?

Then the light was snapped on and Face made the coffee and Harry said: "My dear Mrs. Knight, don't ask me about my baby. I never see her. I shan't feel the slightest interest in her until she has a lover," and Mug took his eye out of the conservatory for a moment and then put it under glass again and Eddie Warren drank his coffee and set down the cup with a face of anguish as though he had drunk and seen the spider.

"What I want to do is to give the young men a show. I believe London is simply teeming with first-chop, unwritten plays. What I want to say to 'em is: 'Here's the theatre. Fire ahead.'"

"You know, my dear, I am going to decorate a room for the Jacob Nathans. Oh, I am so tempted to do a fried-fish scheme, with the backs of the chairs shaped like frying pans and lovely chip potatoes embroidered all over the curtains."

"The trouble with our young writing men is that they are still too romantic. You can't put out to sea without being seasick and wanting a basin. Well, why won't they have the courage of those basins?"

"A *dreadful* poem about a *girl* who was *violated* by a beggar *without* a nose in a lit-tle wood. . . ."

Miss Fulton sank into the lowest, deepest chair and Harry handed round the cigarettes.

From the way he stood in front of her shaking the silver box and saying abruptly: "Egyptian? Turkish? Virginian? They're all mixed up," Bertha realized that she not only bored him; he really disliked her. And she decided from the way Miss Fulton said: "No, thank you, I won't smoke," that she felt it, too, and was hurt.

"Oh, Harry, don't dislike her. You are quite wrong about her. She's wonderful, wonderful. And, besides, how can you feel so differently about someone who means so much to me. I shall try to tell you when we are in bed to-night what has been happening. What she and I have shared."

At those last words something strange and almost terrifying darted into Bertha's mind. And this something blind and smiling whispered to her: "Soon these people will go. The house will be quiet—quiet. The lights will be out. And you and he will be alone together in the dark room—the warm bed. . . ."

She jumped up from her chair and ran over to the piano.

"What a pity someone does not play!" she cried. "What a pity somebody does not play."

For the first time in her life Bertha Young desired her husband.

Oh, she'd loved him—she'd been in love with him, of course, in every other way, but just not in that way. And, equally, of course, she'd understood that he was different. They'd discussed it so often. It had worried her dreadfully at first to find that she was so cold, but after a time it had not seemed to matter. They were so frank with each other—such good pals. That was the best of being modern.

But now—ardently! ardently! The word ached in her ardent

body! Was this what that feeling of bliss had been leading up to? But then, then—

"My dear," said Mrs. Norman Knight, "you know our shame. We are the victims of time and train. We live in Hampstead. It's been so nice."

"I'll come with you into the hall," said Bertha. "I loved having you. But you must not miss the last train. That's so awful, isn't it?"

"Have a whisky, Knight, before you go?" called Harry.

"No, thanks, old chap."

Bertha squeezed his hand for that as she took it.

"Good night, good-bye," she cried from the top step, feeling that this self of hers was taking leave of them for ever.

When she got back into the drawing-room the others were on the move.

". . . Then you can come part of the way in my taxi."

"I shall be *so* thankful *not* to have to face *another* drive *alone* after my *dreadful* experience."

"You can get a taxi at the rank just at the end of the street. You won't have to walk more than a few yards."

"That's a comfort. I'll go and put on my coat."

Miss Fulton moved towards the hall and Bertha was following when Harry almost pushed past.

"Let me help you."

Bertha knew that he was repenting his rudeness—she let him go. What a boy he was in some ways—so impulsive—so—simple.

And Eddie and she were left by the fire.

"I *wonder* if you have seen Bilks' *new* poem called *Table d'Hôte*," said Eddie softly. "It's *so* wonderful. In the last Anthology. Have you got a copy? I'd *so* like to *show* it to you. It begins with an *incredibly* beautiful line: 'Why Must it Always be Tomato Soup?'"

"Yes," said Bertha. And she moved noiselessly to a table opposite the drawing-room door and Eddie glided noiselessly after her. She picked up the little book and gave it to him; they had not made a sound.

While he looked it up she turned her head towards the hall. And she saw . . . Harry with Miss Fulton's coat in his arms and

Miss Fulton with her back turned to him and her head bent. He tossed the coat away, put his hands on her shoulders and turned her violently to him. His lips said: "I adore you," and Miss Fulton laid her moonbeam fingers on his cheeks and smiled her sleepy smile. Harry's nostrils quivered; his lips curled back in a hideous grin while he whispered. "Tomorrow," and with her eyelids Miss Fulton said: "Yes."

"Here it is," said Eddie. " 'Why Must it Always be Tomato Soup?' It's so *deeply* true, don't you feel? Tomato soup is so *dreadfully* eternal."

"If you prefer," said Harry's voice, very loud, from the hall. "I can phone you a cab to come to the door."

"Oh, no. It's not necessary," said Miss Fulton, and she came up to Bertha and gave her the slender fingers to hold.

"Good-bye. Thank you so much."

"Good-bye," said Bertha.

Miss Fulton held her hand a moment longer.

"Your lovely pear tree!" she murmured.

And then she was gone, with Eddie following, like the black cat following the grey cat.

"I'll shut up shop," said Harry, extravagantly cool and collected.

"Your lovely pear tree—pear tree—pear tree!"

Bertha simply ran over to the long windows.

"Oh, what is going to happen now?" she cried.

But the pear tree was as lovely as ever and as full of flower and as still.

Dialogue dominates this story, but Mansfield keeps it under control. These characters are verbally dextrous people who use language to assert their membership in a hip, educated "modern" society. They use slang. They emphasize words for effect, as when Eddie Warren says, "And *in* the moonlight this *bizarre* figure with the *flattened* head *crouching* over the *lit-tle* wheel. . . ." Mansfield establishes Eddie's speech patterns so clearly with his monologue that his lines are rarely tagged in the rest of the story.

Of course, the reader is not supposed to see Bertha, Harry and the gang as educated and modern. To us, they are pretentious and foolish. Mansfield uses the dialogue to drive home this irony. We know almost from the start that Bertha's bliss will come to a bad end. As these people gab away the evening, their silly patter is deepened, made resonant, by our knowledge that Bertha's bubble of self-satisfaction will soon burst.

Take a pen and mark or make a list of all the uses of repetition, interruption, misdirection and any of the other dialogue techniques we've discussed in this book. The key is to examine how a writer uses dialogue in a narrative from start to finish. Give it a try.

ABOUT THE AUTHOR

Tom Chiarella is a member of the English department at DePauw University in Greencastle, Indiana. Born in Rochester, New York, he received a BA from St. Lawrence University and an MFA from the University of Alabama. He is the author of a collection of stories, *Foley's Luck* (Knopf). His fiction and nonfiction have appeared in *The New Yorker, Esquire,* STORY, *The Florida Review* and elsewhere. He has won grants from the NEA and the Indiana Arts Commission. He lives in Greencastle with his wife and two sons.

INDEX